Women of Influence

Stories to Inspire, Encourage, and Empower the Professional Woman

Amber E. Williams
Gigi Brown
Brittany A. Daniel, LPC
Lakichay Nadira Muhammad
Njeri Watkins

Dardon Books

Copyright © Amber E. Williams

All Rights Reserved. No part of this book may be reproduced, stored in a retrieval system, or transmitted by any means without the written permission of the author.

Cover design by LadyMbooks
Simply Edited by Jymyaka Braden

ISBN-13: 978-0-9820973-2-8

Printed in the United States of America

Table of Contents

Introduction 1
Amber E. Williams

Chapter One The New Normal 5
Brittany A. Daniel, LPC

Chapter Two Removing the Masks 15
Star Parker

Chapter Three Leading the Way 23
Njeri Watkins

Chapter Four Why Me? 37
Alycia Richard

Chapter Five Building Boundaries 57
Brittany A. Daniel, LPC

Chapter Six Gold Digger 71
Lakichay Nadira Muhammad

Chapter Seven Self-care in the Process of Change 93
Krystal Humphrey

Chapter Eight State of Mind 99
Gigi Brown

Chapter Nine Unwrapped Gifts: Tapping into the Divine Power Within 109
Lakichay Nadira Muhammad

Chapter Ten The Call for Authentic, Servant Leaders 125
Gigi Brown

Chapter Eleven Depression is a Real Thing 133
Dr. Temeca L. Richardson

Chapter Twelve The Enemy Within 141
Amber E. Williams

About the Authors 187

Introduction

testify: to bear witness

My life has been defined by the many roles that I have taken on--daughter, sister, student, wife, mother, teacher, leader, friend, colleague, mentor, and so many more. With each of these roles, I have experienced things that have defined me, shaped me, wounded me, groomed me, limited me, freed me, and taught me. I understand that these experiences become my stories, but what is a story with no one to tell it to?

I longed to have someone to tell my stories to. I did not know it then, but keeping my stories bottled up only increased my feelings of isolation. The further I climbed up the career ladder, the lonelier I became. I believed that I did not have anyone to tell my stories to that truly understood what I was experiencing and, many times, I felt like I was the only woman in the world to experience these things. After all, no one was sharing their experiences with me that sounded anything like what I was going through. I also didn't want my innermost thoughts and experiences to be held against me. That is exactly what isolation will do to you. I knew what I was feeling could not be the truth, so I decided to open my mouth and speak. In the quiet of offices behind closed doors, in rushed phone conversations on speaker in the car, in off-site lunches at conferences, I began testing the waters by telling parts of my story. These became safe spaces for opening up and other women in my life followed suit. We were not alone. Our stories were not unique. And there was hope on the other side.

    As women in the workplace, there often feels like there is an expectation for us to be superhuman. To share our challenges or painful experiences may seem like a weakness which we cannot afford if we want to compete. I know that I was afraid to show my weakness for fear that someone would try and take my position, discredit me, block me, disrespect me, or any other fear that my mind would think up. I formed a tough exterior which was difficult to penetrate by anyone, but inside I was broken! I began to look around and I saw that I was not the only one.

There were so many broken women around me. I wondered if they needed to open up too.

The realization that we all needed to speak up and testify emboldened me. I encouraged those around me to speak up and to speak out about the good, the bad, and the ugly in our lives. I truly believe that there are other women waiting to hear these stories so that they can be reassured that they can overcome, persevere, and thrive. God laid it upon my heart to compile this book. This collection of stories by amazing professional women who have the courage to speak up about their obstacles and challenges is meant to inspire, encourage, and empower other women. We are not alone, and our stories are powerful.

This is my testimony. This is our testimony.

Amber E. Williams

Chapter One

The New Normal

Redefining Your Standard of Success

Brittany A. Daniel, LPC

Like most know-it-all teenage girls at the age of 15, I pretty much had my whole life figured out. I was going to go to college, get a job, and meet me a tall chocolate mister (you know the Idris Elba type). Of course, "Idris" and I were going to get married, have two kids, adopt a dog, and live in a beautiful two-story home. I was determined to live my life enjoying all of its luxuries. I just knew I was going to be that girl who was young, successful, and at the top of her game.

Thinking back, I can admit it sounds a little made for T.V., but at the time you couldn't tell me otherwise. Like most of us growing up, I wanted to experience the "American Dream." I wanted to experience success and according to the world around me my plans made perfect sense. Society said in order to have success and live this ideal life I had to follow a particular path. I had to go along with the standard that was set before me, or at least that's what I thought.

Whether we'd like to admit it or not, we have all thought along those lines at one point or another. Just take a second and think back. What was the original plan for your life? Whether it was to go to college or to get married, to have kids or not, the point is you had a plan for yourself that was fueled by a desire to attain a certain standard of success. You had an idea of who you wanted to be and how you wanted the world to see you; or at least I know I did. My plans were locked and loaded; however, the one thing I didn't plan for was life in the real world.

The Real World

Reality hit my sophomore year of college when I found myself 19 and pregnant by a man who at the time wanted nothing to do with me. By the age of 20, I was officially a single mother with full-time bills, a part-time job, and now an extra mouth to feed. I was a broke college student, living in the hood depending on government assistance to get by. I was at the bottom and I couldn't stop myself from thinking, "How did I get here?"

I had deviated so far from my ideal life and the standard of what I thought success was that I began to doubt myself. I was discouraged and disappointed in myself. On the outside I felt judged and criticized and on the inside I felt like a failure. Reality had come in and stomped all over my plans and it felt as if I was suffocating under the weight of my circumstances. For a moment I had given up all hope for success simply because things had not gone according to plan.

The Choice to Adapt

With time passing I finally came to accept that my plans had become fragments of what should have been. However, in the midst of that acceptance I decided that I still wanted more for myself. I didn't want to wallow in pity or victimize myself because of my situation. Instead of giving in I came to realize that in order to move forward out of my funk, I would have to take action. In moving forward, I would have to choose to change the course of my life by either adhering or adapting to my current situation.

In adhering I would be choosing to cling to my situation allowing it to not only define me but to dictate the outcome of my life. Along with that, I would be allowing the world around me to weigh in and classify my life as less than ideal. Ultimately, I would be adhering to society's opinions and accepting a life of mediocracy due to my circumstance. In other words, I would be going along to get along.

On the other hand, I could choose to adapt. This would mean reinventing myself despite my circumstance. Adapting would be choosing to pick myself up, brush myself off, and live beyond what was expected of someone in my situation. Instead of giving up my plans I would be reconstructing them by defining my own standard of success and accepting my new NORM-al.

Know No Limits

As a result of going through life's challenges we've all been left with the choice to adhere or to adapt. In other words, we have the power to choose whether to bounce back or not after our plans go astray (and they often do). No matter how hard we try, we can't avoid trials and unexpected setbacks. Despite our efforts we will experience disappointments, delays, and even some denials. We will be told "No" and "You can't" by those who are closest to us. To top it off, society will try to convince us that because of who we are, our obligations, or our circumstances that our dreams and goals are out of reach. The question is, "What do you do in response to that?"

Unless you're willing to just sit back and accept the opinions, labels, and limits imposed by others then at some point you have to be willing to take action. At some point you have to choose to fight back using your adversity as your motivation. Yes, your circumstances and obligations may make things a little more challenging; however, your success lies in your ability to be resilient and your willingness to adapt to your challenges as they come.

Once you choose to adapt you no longer allow your circumstances to define or limit you. Instead, adapting allows you the opportunity to increase positive thinking and to remove any thoughts that could be self-defeating. You know those thoughts that make you believe things like you can't be a wife and head of a company, or that since you didn't graduate college you can't start a business, and my favorite is that you can't have kids and still fulfill your dreams. These are thoughts that limit your innate abilities.

Instead of succumbing to these thoughts and limiting yourself you have to be willing to manifest success inclusive of your circumstances. That's right! Own who you are and your experiences! By owning who you are and your experiences, good and bad, you remove limits and take back your power. When you take ownership you stop caring about the opinions and standards of others, and you start denying people the opportunity to have an impressionable judgment of your life.

For me I had to accept at 19 that I was going to be a mother. I had to own my role, viewing it as an extinction of who I had always been, a young girl with tenacity and a purpose. Of course, this didn't take away from me being uncertain at times, but it did remind me of the strength I had to persevere and push past limits imposed by others, and most importantly imposed by myself.

Accept your New Norm-al

Your situation might not be ideal but that does not take away from the power you have to create the life that you desire. That means yes, you can be a single mother and have a thriving business. And yes, you can be a wife and partner at your firm. The truth is the only one who can determine or dictate what success looks like for you is you.

You are a woman of resource! You are of strength and vitality and cannot be put in a box. Your life might not fall in line with the norm, but it's your norm. It took me a while, but I had to learn to accept this as my truth.

Getting pregnant at 19 and out of wedlock did not constitute success nor was it the ideal standard, however it was my life and it was my new norm. Taking my son to class, juggling work and school, late nights, and early mornings all became a part of my new norm. Was it difficult? Of course! However, my determination was at an all-time high. I had refused to allow my obligation in my role as a single mother stop me from accomplishing my goals. The struggle was real, but before I knew it, I had both my bachelor's and master's degrees. I had become a licensed counselor, a business owner, an author, and a homeowner. I still hadn't found my Idris, but I wasn't complaining. The point is I created success with my circumstance literally on my hip at every turn. When society was ready to label me a statistic I chose to live as the exception.

Create your Own Standard

Maybe things didn't go according to plan. So, what! My challenge to you is to accept who you are and live as the exception. You are right where you need to be with all of the tools you need to move forward, unless you decide not to. Therefore, be the woman who refuses to be defined. Set your own standard based on your lifestyle and the things that are important to you.

Instead of being intimidated by all that you are, use that as a source of inspiration and strength. Understand that every challenge, circumstance or hardship that you have overcome has deposited courage and zeal within you. Embrace your role as mother, sister, wife, and boss chick. Instead of being confined by societal standards be brave enough to create your own.

Chapter Two

Removing the Masks

Reminder to Self: The Best Me is All I Need to Be

Star Parker

Everything in my gut urged me to go to my assigned high school on this particular day and I'm thankful I listened to that voice. I reluctantly dismissed the invitation of my high school "friends" to skip and hang out at the neighborhood school, which was normally a part of our regularly scheduled day. Once I got to school, my teachers and classmates had a slew of questions about where I had been most of the school year. Everyone was surprised to see me in class. Some of their sarcastic comments made it more uncomfortable for me to stay a full day than I imagined. My anxiety was through the roof and, though I contemplated leaving, I made it through the day.

I remember the child who once greeted every school morning with anticipation because that was the one place I stood out as the head of the class, the one place I was comfortable in my own skin and proud to be considered "different from the rest." In elementary school, I was ecstatic every time one of my teachers would assign me to help my fellow classmates who struggled to complete their classwork on their own. I would complete each assignment as fast and accurately as I could, anticipating my opportunity to be the assigned assistant for the day.

Then there was that time I scored way above average on the citywide test and several school officials came to meet with my teachers and I to investigate whether I may have cheated to obtain such high grades. Even if I was a tad annoyed by the gesture, the thought that my scores demanded such attention was paramount. This stirred up a feeling of confidence in me and I was on a mission. Despite the constant reaffirmations to work hard in school, land a job in the medical field, acquire a position as a school teacher or a career in the likeness of, I wanted to own things, create, and build monopolies. I knew I was born to be different.

By the time I reached the 6th grade, my family moved to a new community and I noticed quickly that the school atmosphere was much different than I was used to. I rushed to complete my work, as usual, raised my hand to answer questions, and took pride in being knowledgeable. I soon learned that being considered the teacher's pet wasn't cool and trust me, I found out the hard way.

As if being considered a "kiss up" wasn't enough, I also dressed differently, often times not matching and wearing clothing I felt was a reflection of my creativity. Being bullied and teased became a part of my daily routine. My classmates described me as "weird" and as much as I liked being different, I despised being ridiculed for it.

One day at the water fountain with my head down, I overheard a few of my classmates telling a girl I once considered a friend to push me. I didn't bother to look up knowing she would never listen to them. After being hit from behind and after a fight I couldn't remember, we were both suspended. I plead my case adamantly. She started the fight and I acted in self-defense.

Several fights later, fighting as if my life depended on it, I was suspended more times than I care to recount. There were a couple suspensions I was able to talk myself out of due to the fact I never initiated any of the fights.

Soon, tables began to turn and I became popular for beating my opponents. I was now greeted with a different type of acceptance and I liked it. I was once again calling the shots. I became the bully nobody wanted beef with. I was considered one of the most popular and I liked it because this meant I didn't have to fight anymore. It seemed people finally realized I was a force to be reckoned with. I played the part at school, but at home, I felt like a fraud. Becoming someone I didn't recognize, didn't like and didn't want to relate to, became painstakingly more difficult than being the person who was often taunted. I wanted out, but too many people were counting on me to play my new position and being a teenager can be challenging.

There was a city-wide walkout scheduled amongst high school students and of course, I was going. While walking with what seemed to be several hundred students, there was a voice calling my name which got louder as the group of junior high school students pushed their way through the crowd. The young lady who identified herself as my little sister pointed out someone who was threatening to beat her up. I confronted the girl who was clearly older than both of us and was aggressively met with vulgar language. With the crowd egging me on, I threw the first blow. She hit me back and I blacked out. I could hear her pleading for me to stop. I could also hear the crowd cheering me on. Not only was this mot my fight, I also threw the first punch and I was sick about the way I behaved. There was a lot of talk about me winning the fight, but it seemed nobody knew I was losing the battle inside.

I prayed and cried that whole weekend, asking for forgiveness and making vows to change. I was tired of wearing masks with fake smiles that didn't last. I was exhausted. The next Monday morning I woke up ready to go to school and turn over a new leaf. Before I made it out the door, my phone was blowing up. The invitations to meet up were tempting and though I couldn't bring myself to tell my cut partners I wouldn't be joining them that day, I made my way to school. Later that evening I found out school officials and police were looking to speak with me about the altercation that happened the past Friday. Being obedient and going to school possibly saved me from some serious repercussions and, although I know I was wrong, I am forever grateful for God's mercy.

Sometimes the fearful little girl filled with anxiety and the tendency to escape in times of opposition appears and I must remind myself Who I am and Whose I am. Obstacles and temptations are strategically timed and customized to halt our progress on the course to destiny. These obstacles and temptations disguise themselves by changing their masks and lurking in the shadows, anticipating ownership of one's disgruntled soul.

As Women, Mothers, Wives, Entrepreneurs, etc., we become complacent with the thought of being "Super Women." Though playing different positions may require us to wear different hats, we must be mindful that what we presume to be hats aren't disguises requiring us to juggle masks, for some masks become permanent.

Matthew 16:26
For What is a man profited, if he shall gain the world, and lose his own soul?

Chapter Three
Leading the Way

Njeri Watkins

Embracing Uncertainty

I was no longer working from home, I was home in my work. I was eleven months into my entrepreneurial journey as Consultant and Facilitator. My business had become my healthy obsession. My daily routine had evolved into four parts business activities, one part personal development, and one part spiritual enlightenment.

There would be moments of pure bliss followed by a driving curiosity of what do I do next? How do I plan with so much uncertainty? How could I stabilize my structures so that I could work in my zone of excellence and be of greater value to the world and marketplace? I was sharp and sound in my work but seeking a structured plan or roadmap that could incorporate my expertise with who I was authentically.

I was on a solo journey that often left me alone, yet I was never lonely. It is here where I would experience the depths of my soul, explore the capabilities of my mind, and nurture the facets of my creativity. I was tapping into something within myself that was totally invigorating to no end. It was an essence that I felt but I didn't have a clue on how to cultivate this energy into something tangible.

My world had evolved into an existence that no longer fit into the confines of what was familiar in my lived experience. I felt closeted and couldn't figure out why. I felt guilty for no longer sharing the same values and interests in things that connected me with people and environments of the past. I could no longer engage in basic conversations like the weather forecast, nightly news, or fear-based, media-driven conversations.

Igniting the Productive Disruptor Within

I was existing in a state that I would later refer to as "productive disruption". I was embarking on some deep work while simultaneously holding space in two worlds--the delicate dance of entrepreneurship, forever existing in the present and future. This required an enormous amount of mental bandwidth causing my energy to wane.

The unfoldment of something beautiful was being birthed but I couldn't name it or claim it in the physical world. I felt anxious and on the cusp of something big but didn't know how to get there or what to do. I felt compelled to recalibrate and reorganize my life. This grew into a slight frustration to the point where I needed a break but not an escape, simply a quiet place away where I could reflect.

I would soon find myself traveling over to the island to visit a retreat center for individual retreatants seeking spiritual renewal, respite, and growth. After three days of peaceful solitude without technology, I would come up for air and secretly browse YouTube and return my text messages and emails. A holistic life coach appeared on YouTube with a message that spoke to me. The phone number in the description link was a local area code and for the next hour I engaged in a transformational discussion on work life synergy, energetic constitution, and B.E.S.T. (Bio Energetic Synchronization Technique).

The BEST Kept Secret

I was eager to work with this coach to learn a holistic modality of integrating the facets of my inner self and physical life according to my evolved beliefs, values, and desires. I was thrilled to be getting started and the next several weeks I did "the work". For the first time in my life I conducted a detailed life audit of all the significant incidents, experiences, achievements, and relationships in my life from birth. One by one I analyzed each item and reflected on how it impacted my beliefs, values, desires, and future actions. I was able to glean a myriad of insights about my life, my behavior and my interactions with others that would forever change the way I viewed purpose and reason for being here on earth.

This significant investment in holistic personal development had no immediate impact on daily activities or business pursuits. However, the deep work I was embarking on empowered me to own every aspect of my life while fostering substantial growth in emotional intelligence. The additional education on how the body, mind, and soul worked in alignment taught me how our physical world is just a function of this integration. I was fascinated with this newfound knowledge and committed to building on this wisdom in ongoing activities in developing my own selfcare practice.

I absolutely loved doing "the work" but would find it frustrating and uncomfortable when I would experience friction from existing relationships and individuals who challenged my progression. Some of my relationships and activities I engaged in were simply out of habit or unconsciously egoic in nature that satisfied a belief or an outcome that no longer resonated with me.

As I continued to do the work, I noticed I had expanded my energetic and emotional capacity. I soon realized the power I had inside to really own my emotions, thoughts, and feelings and not feel bound by the impact of collective engagements I was a part of. I could no longer be triggered into old conversations, behaviors, and actions just because they were familiar.

The Real Magic Revealed

My new-found awareness would forever alter how I engaged and experienced the world. I was consciously creating the environment around me and no longer unconsciously living in reaction to the events and circumstances in my life. I learned that it was possible to experience an emotion without letting that emotion dictate or dominate future behavior and actions. Emotions and feelings were no longer random and need not be feared or hidden. I watched as I could feel, express, and share without the need for attachment or acknowledgement.

As my level of self-acceptance and awareness expanded so did my analytical skills. I was able to recognize patterns or trends quickly and easily identify outliers. I intuitively knew the next steps I needed to take would not be in my existing environment or frame of reference. I could no longer go through life as I once did, quietly acquiescing to my existing environment and social morays or conforming for the sake of habit. This ultimately led to my next challenge of redefining who I was and how I showed up in the world.

Defining Who You Are and How You Show Up in the World

A strong voice within spoke to me, "Njeri, you don't fit in and that is not your lot in life. You create the space for others to fit in. That is what you do authentically. Your divinity and true essence is expressed through your leadership." This was my truth. At that moment I felt 100% in alignment with this truth and welcomed this part of my identity.

Regardless of who I was with or where I was at, I was always in some form creating the space and leading. All my fond memories, significant achievements, and close relationships were all born out of my ability to create a space that would nurture expansion and development which enabled people to feel validated and be reminded of their true potential. Whether it was through my teaching, consulting or speaking, all roads would lead back to the same outcome.

The irony is that this roadmap or plan I once believed I needed led me on this journey back to myself. I had come full circle and it all was making perfect sense. I was ready to own my life in a way like never before. I began expanding my consulting work to include aspects of personal development and life lessons I experienced when it was appropriate to do so. I began to openly acknowledge and recognize the personal growth and subtle changes of others that often go unnoticed. As I continued to evolve, so did my work, relationships, and environments and the opportunities that came forth. I would soon begin receiving requests to mentor young adults and teach on topics outside of my professional expertise such as soft skill development, leadership, and empowerment.

There was a depth on an emotional, mental and spiritual level that really allowed for greater understanding and connection with others. This led to me being invited to places and spaces with other lifelong learners investing in activities and education in pursuit of becoming the best version of themselves in their personal and professional lives.

Leading Fearlessly

It was a pretty surreal moment when I walked through the door to teach my first class with the Continuing Studies at the University of British Columbia (UBC). I had been a guest speaker a number of times prior in this very room, but to teach a course in the new Social Media program was a significant milestone in year three of my entrepreneurial journey.

An hour into the class I encountered what would be every presenter's biggest nightmare—a disgruntled student who starts a hostile takeover of the class. Out of nowhere came a litany of rapid-fire questions that were outside the objectives of the course and more suitably answered by a cybersecurity lawyer. While some of her concerns were legitimate outside the scope of this course, the abrasive tone and aggressive nature sparked a series of rants from other students. This snowballed into a heated discussion on how disruptive and unproductive social media is in their lives and society as a whole.

Of all the presentations and courses I have delivered over the years, what would be the chances that this would be the one class that I would have to experience the most public humiliation and distress? This class was being audited by three of UBC leadership teams and the Program Leader who engaged me as an instructor. For the first time in my life I was at a loss for words and devastated that my new role as a UBC Instructor was fait accompli in less than ninety minutes.

Trusting the Process

It would turn out that even with this disruptive first class, I received exceptionally favorable evaluations from the students. To my surprise, I was invited to teach in the UBC Life and Career Program by the Director who had audited the course. On the outside I appeared to have everything under control and handled the situation well. However, this was the most challenging class I had ever taught and learned an invaluable lesson in the process--the importance of being able to handle conflict and distressing situations in real time. This is what comes with the responsibility of being a leader.

I decided to level up and started placing myself in environments where I would have the opportunity to practice high level crucial conversations in real time. I enrolled in the Facilitative Leadership Program through Executive Education at University of Victoria where I was able to train and role play with CEO's, Senior Executives from some of the top organizations in the province. I registered for a negotiation course as well as a Communicate with Confidence program.

Even though I had completed an Instructor Certification and had been facilitating for years prior, these programs pushed me past my comfort zone to further develop my skills and take my role as Instructor to the next level. I learned how to unapologetically own the room by setting boundaries for class, hone in on my authentic teaching method to lead the conversation, and become comfortable in engaging in crucial conversations when the stakes are right.

The Gift of Growth

There was a time when I hoped and prayed for a smooth ride through life wanting everything to work out according to plan while living an existence that kept everything manageable and in perfect harmony. Today, I live a life where no two days are close to the same and I fully embrace uncertainty on a regular basis. It has been through the space of possibility where the true gifts of the entrepreneurial journey have been revealed.

Over time I learned to view the obstacles in my life, not as things to be avoided, but as a series of events that I am privileged to experience for the purpose of garnering a deeper understanding and love for myself and the human experience. It is through facing these challenges that I have come to appreciate the real meaning of life experienced in those ever-so-precious encounters. The courage to do this has meant experiences, emotions, connections, and blessings that have expanded my capacity to understand, love, and connect with others.

As I enter my 10th year as a UBC Instructor, I truly hold the learning environment sacred as it is where I have experienced most of my silent victories and witnessed the many priceless moments of truth and understandings of my students. This has equipped me to harness a deeper connection and understanding of the human potential in others and to truly support them in defining who they really are and how they show up in the world.

Ubuntu.
Njeri Watkins

Chapter Four
Why Me?

Alycia Richard

The saying goes that when God is ready to take you to another level, He will make you uncomfortable in your current situation. Well, I was definitely uncomfortable and in a place where I didn't have anyone to depend on but God! I had worked with physicians in one capacity or another for ten years. Historically, I had never experienced any conflicts with any of my previous bosses. As a matter of fact, I took pride in being able to successfully work with the physicians that had a reputation for being difficult. One day that all changed, and I found myself at a spiritual crossroads that would change the course of my life forever.

I began as a Unit Secretary in the Emergency Center of a pediatric hospital. As my career progressed, so did my level of education and I was budding with optimism about my future career possibilities. Within a year of completing my bachelor's degree, I had given birth to my second child and landed a well-paying position with one of the most prestigious departments in the hospital. There, I provided administrative support to five clinicians and three post-doctoral faculty members. I became the "go-to" person to resolve just about any issue that arose in the office. Things were good, and I was happy. One day I received an email regarding a position that would be coming available in one of the other departments. The position was a mid-level leadership role as a Graduate Medical Education (GME) program coordinator. Although I was ready to advance into a leadership role, I was comfortable in my role at the time. I actually had my eyes on my supervisor's job and I was willing to bide my time and continue to make a name for myself until my then supervisor retired. Uninterested, I forwarded the email advertising the program coordinator position to one of my coworkers who was in search of another job. My co-worker was offered the coordinator position, but by what seemed to be a twist of fate, she declined the offer and decided to accept a different role. After going on and on about how much she thought I would be the perfect fit for the coordinator role, she encouraged me to apply for the position. I did and a month after interviewing, I was thriving in my new role, which felt like my dream job.

Being hired as the Program Coordinator made me feel as though I was on the right track in my career. I knew that I wanted to advance in the field of graduate medical education and within my first few months of employment I decided to pursue my master's degree. Although there was a lot to learn about my new role, the institution I worked for had no formal training for this position whatsoever. Each department had its own program coordinator and we helped one another as much as possible, but because each department operated differently, I had to learn a lot through trial and error. The Program Director and Assistant Program Director were very helpful. They were both subspecialty clinicians who graduated from the same program they were now in charge of. Both were very much invested in the legacy and overall success of the program and gave me the freedom to make things my own to catapult the program to the next level.

For the first year everything was great, and I was really good at my job. My primary responsibilities were to coordinate recruitment, onboard new trainees, and plan graduation. The other supervisors made me feel as though my ideas and input were a valuable asset to the team. Now that I look back, I realize that there were times that I picked up a little tension between myself and the Program Director, however, I attributed this to our cultural differences. I believed we would resolve them over time the more we got to know one another. Fortunately, the Assistant Director seemed to understand the both of us very well and was there to balance out the team.

In the middle of my first year, we had a trainee that was struggling in the program and we all had different opinions about how we should handle the situation. The Program Director immediately began putting things in place to create a paper trail on this trainee to support their removal from the program. The Assistant Director and I thought that removal should be a last resort and we wanted to do everything possible to help the trainee make it through the program. Nevertheless, the director was relentless and convinced the program board that something had to be done about the trainee because the reputation of the program was at stake. She decided that the Assistant Director and I would be responsible for overseeing a 6-week remediation plan while she would be out on a medical sabbatical. We both voiced our disapproval of this approach, but in the end the board voted in her favor. This was the first time that our team didn't feel like a team anymore.

While she was out on sabbatical, I was the primary person running the program. The Assistant Director was there for support if needed, however, everything fell on me because he had a very large patient load. The other trainees and some of the faculty members were very concerned about the struggling trainee and did not agree with the remediation approach either. They all voiced their opinions to me as the official representative of the program. I answered as many questions as I could to the best of my abilities while maintaining confidentiality and respecting the sensitivity of the struggling trainee's situation. One day, while the director was still out on sabbatical, the section chief called my supervisor and I into his office and questioned me about things that were going on with the trainee and the remediation plan. I answered each question honestly and for the questions that I didn't have the answers to, I encouraged him to contact the program director directly. After meeting with the section chief, I called the director and informed her of our meeting. The director was immediately angry with me and accused me of spreading gossip. I was shocked and totally confused by her response. I asked her if I had done something that she didn't approve of, but she told me that it if anyone has any questions about anything dealing with the program they need to call her on her cell phone even though she was out on medical sabbatical. Upset and confused, I informed the Assistant Director about the conversation I had with the director and he said … "I don't think you did anything wrong, that's just how she is sometimes." I took his word that I had not done anything inappropriate and moved on.

At that time our program was on a down season. One of the other coordinators had informed me about a process improvement course that was being offered by the institution. She informed me that the objective of the course was to learn to remove waste from processes and solve problems caused by processes that ultimately cost the organization money. Upon completion of the course I would be responsible for completing a project that implemented the methodologies to earn an official certification. I had never heard of the program nor did I know that there was a certification that could be attained for improving processes. However, taking the course felt like a no brainer since the cost was fully absorbed by the institution and I was already improving the processes of our program. I figured since we were on a down season and the program director was out on a medical sabbatical, I might as well get certified to do what I was already doing so well.

When the director returned from her sabbatical her attitude was not the same. During our weekly meetings (and even when we interacted with one another in general) the overall energy just felt different than before. It felt as though we were all trying to "play nice" but we had not resolved or even discussed the issues we had with the way things had been handled. Ultimately, the program board voted to remove the struggling trainee from the program. Not too long after, the Assistant Director announced that he would be resigning from the program. From there, my relationship with the program director began on an irreparable downward spiral.

The following year things got even worse. What began as little small awkward moments turned into full on avoidance and childish passive aggressive behavior. For example, we had bi-weekly lunch-and-learn sessions for the trainees. Before, she would roll up her sleeves to help me clean the conference rooms and transport the leftover food back to our office after the meetings. She had gotten to the point where she would not lift a finger to help with anything and would bark orders at me as if I were her personal hired domestic helper. I felt like she was going out of her way to belittle me and assert her authority over me to *put me in my place* so to speak. Although our weekly meetings continued, they were no longer the collaborative planning sessions that I had grown to love. When I presented ideas or suggestions, she would make degrading comments like, "I know this is a hard concept for you to understand," or "I believe you think you are more than what you really are." Eventually, I began to wonder if the things she was saying about me were true.

At this point I knew for certain that something was wrong, and I was determined to figure out how to fix things between the two of us. At the time, I believed that God had blessed me with this job, so it was up to me to make it work. I decided that the best course of action was for me to work harder and to make the program bigger and better by going above and beyond what was expected of me. I'd be at work some nights until midnight working to make things great. I neglected my children and my own needs to make improvements to this program while my program director was at home enjoying her children and her family. Any attempt on my part to make things better between us just wasn't enough. Every late hour went unnoticed. No matter what I said or did, there was nothing that I could do to get things back to how they were before.

Year three was the absolute worst. In addition to the growing tension at work, I was separating from my husband of ten years. I was in the process of moving my children from our personal home to my parents' house on the other side of town. I was uprooting my daughter from her school and her friends. Although my dad had assured me that everything would work out, this was an extremely stressful time for me. When I shared this news with the program director, she was not at all concerned about how I was coping with this major life transition, nor did she ask how my children were handling things. Although her attitude had been gradually changing towards me, I expected her to respond with some sort of compassion or sensitivity for my situation from one woman (better yet wife and mother) to another. She offered no support. Instead, she looked at me with cold, judgmental eyes and said, "Do whatever you need to do."

I didn't realize the depth of the director's contempt for me until I had completed my master's program and submitted a request to my supervisor for a promotion. To my surprise, just like with the struggling trainee, the director began building a paper trail to support my termination. She submitted a letter to my supervisor insisting that I be written up for unreasonable infractions that occurred during the previous year. The director and my supervisor were both fully aware of the minor infractions when they occurred, and they were not an issue at the time. However, the director framed everything in a way that made me look bad on paper. My supervisor agreed that the write up was not necessary; However, her hands were tied because the director had spoken to the section chief and insisted that my supervisor add the documentation to my personnel file. In addition to the write up, the director did everything in her power to remove the enjoyable components of my job. She knew how much I enjoyed recruitment, but she took that responsibility away from me. She forced my supervisor to assign recruitment to one of the administrative team members who was not interested nor qualified to do the job. I asked the director repeatedly, "What am I doing wrong? How can I make this better?" The only response I ever received was, "You are great at what you do but we just have a personality conflict." I was astonished! As my superior I felt as though the director should be the one to set the tone in our work relationship and I would follow her lead. I didn't understand how we could possibly have a personality conflict. Even when I tried to be the bigger person and take the lead in turning things around for us, she would push me away. It had gotten so bad that I called the HR department and informed them of what was going on. I was afraid that I would lose my job which absolutely could not happen because I was the sole breadwinner and caretaker of my children. The HR representative empathized with my situation but informed me that unfortunately the director has the right to run the program as she sees fit which includes hiring and terminating program staff. She encouraged me to begin updating my resume and apply to other internal job postings. Meantime, I should pretty much do what I could to stay out of the director's way until I find something else.

I was hurt, confused, and doubting myself and I began experiencing migraines for the first time ever. When I was first hired, I loved going to work! I loved my job and I rarely missed a day. During that last year I cried on the way to work just about every morning. I'd arrive to the garage in enough time to make it to the office on time, but I would have to take an additional 15-20 minutes in the car to try to fix my face. So, I was actually arriving to work late most days. I was an absolute mess! One day, my supervisor called me into her office and told me that she understands that I am going through a lot, but I would have to start getting to the office on time or things would get worse. How could I? I didn't even want to be there. During recruitment season I felt like a puppy who had an accident in the house and someone was rubbing my nose in my own mess to teach me a lesson. I was lost. I allowed a job to define and validate me. Without it, who was I? What was I supposed to do? How would I move forward? I just wanted to know, why me? Sure, I was angry at my program director for the way she handled things. More importantly, I was angry at myself for not knowing what to do. That day I asked my supervisor to fire me. I figured if I had gotten fired I could at least collect unemployment benefits to support my kids and not be in such a hostile work environment. Obviously, she refused because there were no grounds to terminate me that would allow me to collect unemployment benefits. I knew that I wouldn't receive unemployment if I quit my job, so I was stuck in a tough and uncomfortable position. I was at an all-time low and it was at that very moment that I realized that I did not have anyone to turn to that could make this right but God!

I remember calling my mom one morning on the way to work and with tears in my eyes saying, "Mom please pray for me. I can't even put the words together to pray for myself." As a mother I can only imagine how my mom felt to hear me in that state. I don't remember what she said, but a peace just began to overcome me on my way in to work that morning. When we hung up all I could say is I give it to you Lord and I began singing *"I surrender all, I surrender all, all to thee my blessed savior, I surrender all."*

I decided that I would put all my efforts into finding another job. I found online courses that helped me tweak my resume and I began applying to anything that came my way. I began applying to a lot of project coordinator and project management roles. Then I realized that I hadn't been selected for any interviews, because I didn't have the proper certifications for the jobs I was applying for. I had no idea how I was going to pay for any certifications because I didn't have the money for it. Then it dawned on me that I had not completed my certification project because I was putting all my efforts into the program. At that time my focus shifted, and I stopped applying to jobs and begin drafting ideas for my certification project. While I was finalizing my project presentation, I received an email informing me that the next certification class would be starting up within a month. I wasn't being utilized in my role and had loads of free time on my hands during the day. I talked to my supervisor and asked If I could continue to work on my presentation during my down time and attend the course when the time comes. She agreed, and I received my certification in enough time to attend the certification course.

A couple of months after I completed the certification course, my supervisor called me into her office to go over my annual evaluation. I received great evaluation scores as usual and she told me that she was proud of the way I had handled things with the program director. She also told me that the director wants another program coordinator and that I would be switching roles with one of the young ladies in the clinic. When she first told me about this, I was surprised but relieved at the same time. Before knowing the full extent of my new responsibilities, I asked her if this could be a permanent switch because I did not feel comfortable working with the director and my supervisor agreed.

I knew that working in the clinic would be a huge demotion in responsibilities for me, however, my salary would not be affected whatsoever! I realized that this was a blessing in disguise and an opportunity for me to continue to grow professionally so I decided to make the best of the situation and find a way to get what I needed out of my new role. The Practice Manager and my new supervisor wanted to meet with me before I transitioned into the clinic role to set expectations and assure me that they were looking forward to having me in the clinic. During our meeting, I informed the manager that I had completed the certification course and I was looking for a project to work on that would allow me to analyze a lot of data so that I could receive my certification. Her eyes lit up with excitement when I told her of my career ambitions and she said that there are lots of project opportunities in the clinic and she would fully support any project that I wanted to work on. In addition to my regular responsibilities, she offered me the opportunity to act as a mini project manager for the clinic where I would be allowed protected days to work only on projects and anything I needed to complete my certification. I wanted to jump through the roof when I received this news because I realized that what someone meant for evil against me God meant it for my good!

I have learned so many lessons during my time of discomfort. Although I am still in the learning process, I am at a point where I can look back and see how much I have grown. I spent a lot of time soul searching, studying and reading trying to understand who I am and how to define myself outside of my job or being a wife, mother, sister or daughter. I wanted to know what makes me, me. Why did I stay in that role for so long? Why did I blame myself for the issues that were going on with the director? Why was I so adamant about fixing the problem myself and more importantly why did I prioritize a job over the health and wellbeing of my family and myself? The more I searched, the more I realized that the way I handled my issues with the program director is the same way I handled the issues in my failing marriage. I realize that I accepted and enabled poor behavior because I didn't know my worth. I was insecure and allowed past mistakes to mold the version of myself that I presented to the world. Because of my insecurities, I held myself to a level of perfection that I would never be able to attain. Worse of all, I didn't believe that I deserved anything more than I had already received which is why I settled for good enough. For a long time, my identity moved with the wind until I finally stopped looking to myself but began looking to my source. For me that source is Jesus Christ and through him I am a child of the Most High God. Through this situation my relationship with God has grown to depths that I would have never imagined, which makes all of the trials that I have experienced worth it. I began to see God's perspective and view of me his child through the lenses of a parent. I learned that since I was created in God's image I inherited his characteristics, so I AM creative and talented, I AM brilliant and special, and I AM beautiful and graceful. I AM NOT perfect because I'm human, but I AM enough and as the daughter of the Most High King I am able to boldly acknowledge that I deserve the best! Once I learned who God is, I learned who I am, and I made a promise to myself that I will always seek God first in everything I do. I will listen for his soft still voice and I will never allow anything or anyone other than him to define or validate me again.

When you find yourself asking "why me" (and trust me at some point in life you will), just remember that God prunes us so that we are able produce more fruit. The pruning process does not feel good and can be really hard for us to understand, but if we will change our perspective and shift our attention away from the pain to focus on God, we will find peace and strength in knowing that everything God does or allows is always for our good. Even though it doesn't feel like it, He is always in the midst of everything working things out for our good because He loves us all.

Be encouraged!

Chapter Five
Building Boundaries
It's Business and Personal

Brittany A. Daniel, LPC

In my opinion Whitney Houston is one of the most iconic female artists of all time. With hits like "I Will Always Love You," and "Heartbreak Hotel" it's really no comparing her. Growing up, one of my favorite Whitney songs was "I'm Every Woman." With the up-tempo beat and the catchiness of the chorus it was undeniably a female anthem. The crazy thing is as much as I liked the song I never payed attention to the words beyond the chorus. It wasn't until about a year ago that I really tuned in and realized that Whitney was tripping. With the lyrics "anything you want done baby, I'll do it naturally," it was clear that Whitney was doing the most. I mean maybe it's just me, but being "every woman" sounded like a full-time job with little to no benefits therefore I was no longer interested.

Now of course I was taking the song out of context but the more I listened the more I couldn't help but wonder how many women actually saw this as an ideal standard to live up to. How many women were aiming to be "every woman", taking on multiple roles and responsibilities simply because it was in their nature? If I were to guess I would say a good majority.

To be truthful I wouldn't be surprised because as women we pride ourselves on being able to do it all. We are high achievers who in recent years have literally taken the phrase "booked and busy" to a whole different level. No longer are we comfortable being limited by labels like mom or wife, instead we strive to be present in every facet. We want to be seen as business moguls and entrepreneurs. We want to be advocates in our community and nurturers to our children. We want to be a refuge for our husband and a shoulder for our friends. We want to be everything for everybody, even if that means neglecting ourselves.

Now don't get me wrong, as women we are more than capable of fulfilling multiple roles and wearing multiple hats. However. what happens when those roles start to require more than what was anticipated? What happens when wanting to be "every woman" seems like less of a choice and becomes more of a chore?

The Realm of Over Commitment

When you aim to be everything for everybody you can easily be sucked into the realm of over commitment, a place plagued with stress, anxiety and un-fulfillment. Unfortunately, this is a place that a lot of women frequent as repeat offenders. We overcommit when it comes to our jobs, our kids, our families, and friends not realizing the internal toll it takes on us. Although our hearts are pure and our motives are selfless, when we take on too much we subject ourselves to being physically, mentally, and emotionally over run.

Being immersed in the world of mental health, this is something that I see every day especially with my female clients. Of course, all of them have unique stories and situations; however, almost all of them share the same complaint of having an excessive amount of stress. These are women like you and I who have careers, goals, and are often seen as the pillars in their families. They are helpers and take pride in their ability to "have it all together." These are compassionate and strong women who unfortunately put themselves last. As a result, they are overworked, overloaded, and often overwhelmed. Their stress and anxiety are at an all-time high because they can't seem to move away from the realm of over commitment.

Balance and Boundaries

It may be hard to believe but the majority of stress is self-sustained by an inability to acknowledge limits and set appropriate boundaries. In other words, we have a hard time turning down people and obligations when they come barreling our way. Instead of drawing a line we over commit ourselves knowing good and well that we don't have the time, resources, and sometimes the mental capacity to take on the task at hand. In our humanistic effort to not disappoint others we subject ourselves to personal inconvenience.

Take a former client of mine for example. She had two small children both under the age of 10 and had recently took in her adult nephew. She was in the process of trying to save for her first home, however she was paying her mother's bills in addition to her own. To top it off she had recently took on a new position at her job that was more work with no increase in pay.

I can remember her coming into my office and describing how depressed, and anxious she was. She was stressed and overwhelmed and it was no surprise why. She was exporting so much of herself while very little was being imported. She was giving and giving with no replenishment and as a result her mental and emotional health were being affected. Now on the outside this was a strong educated woman who was more than capable of seeing all of these commitments through, however the question is, at what cost?

As women the goal is to have ambition and desire however it's important to also have balance and boundaries. We have to be aware of our personal ratio of self-sacrifice to self-fulfillment. If at any time we are sacrificing more for others and not taking the time to assess and replenish ourselves then something needs to change. If not, we will get burnt out and eventually feel depleted.

Build Better Fences

To minimize those feelings of being overwhelmed we have to learn to draw a line in the sand. We have to be able to identify those moments where we begin to lose ourselves and at that point we must choose to create intentional boundaries, aka "build better fences." When you "build fences" or create boundaries you temporarily block out the noise and distractions around you, allotting yourself the opportunity to attend to your own needs and to experience growth.

I once read in a poem that "good fences make good neighbors." Now there are multiple interpretations of this phrase but the one I agree with most is that, when boundaries are clear situations can thrive. Good fences or boundaries remove any contention or debate on where to draw the line. They allow you to prioritize what's important and handpick your commitments. They allow you to decline things outside of your personal preference which makes room for you to engage in those things that will lead to your breakthrough.

When we fail to build those boundaries we can find ourselves overloaded with other people's responsibilities. So much so that when we are presented with an opportunity that would benefit ourselves we miss out because the time and resources that were reserved for us have been distributed amongst everyone else.

This is something that I recently fell victim to myself. Over the past year it had become clear that I was committing myself more to my job than I was to growing my business. In my mind working long hours and late nights for a well-known company appeared to be the right thing to do because it provided financial security. On the other hand, it minimized the opportunity for my business to thrive which left me feeling unfulfilled. I came to realize that there was a lack of balance that limited my potential. Yes, my business was growing but it was not flourishing and it was because I was more committed to maintaining someone else's success rather than nurturing my own.

It was not until I decided to create balance that I noticed a change. Once I decided to allocate time and resources for my business instead of being overloaded with work, things took off. I quickly learned that "good fences" or boundaries were essential in becoming the woman I had desired to be.

Building Boundaries = Self-care

Without balance and boundaries you can easily slip into a place of distress where you feel as if you can barely keep your head above water. For most of us this is where we start looking for some sort of external escape. We start looking outside of ourselves for refuge and comfort not realizing the various self-care strategies that could be used to reduce stress and eliminate those negative feeling. Now I can admit that engaging in self-care can initially feel selfish; however, it's essential to develop this healthy habit in order to fulfill your role as the woman you were intended to be.

Learn to say NO

One of the first strategies that you can implement to help create boundaries and reduce stress is to engage in the self-care act of saying no. That's right, saying no is self-care! Now this does not mean that you should be nasty or dismissive, but instead you should be decisive and honest with yourself regarding your limitations.

For me being able to say no used to be extremely hard because I pride myself on being someone others can depend on. I didn't want to disappoint my friends or family and honestly saying no would make me feel guilty for some odd reason. It wasn't until I noticed that everyone around me was living their best life while I was at a standstill. I was in a place of stagnation when it came to my personal goals and I didn't know why. Once again, I was investing so much of myself into other people that I was neglecting my own desires. Yes, I was helping others, but I was not growing and that alone was one of the most frustrating feelings.

In learning to say no it put me back in position of priority. Instead of being "every woman" for everyone else it allowed me to focus more energy inward to meet my personal needs. I found this to be essential because the only way I could be anything for anyone else was for me to first be 100% within myself.

Saying no creates a space for you to honor your own needs and desires. It "reclaims your time" by creating healthy boundaries and maximizing your availability. By saying no, you create the opportunity to say yes to the things that matter most.

Think before you commit

Another self-care strategy that is helpful in implementing boundaries is to think before you commit. I know this sounds elementary but the truth is a lot of us make commitments without hesitation. In an effort to please others we say yes and agree to obligations without giving it a second thought. Next thing you know, we are knee deep in a situation that we didn't want to be in in the first place. Instead of kicking ourselves once we reach hindsight, it's important to think before we commit.

If someone ask you to do something or invites you to take on a task there is nothing wrong with giving yourself time to consider all factors. Statements such as, "I will let you know," or "Give me a day to think it over," can make all the difference. By giving yourself that time it allows you the opportunity to consider your priorities and put things into perspective. Thinking before you commit allows you the time to assess your current situation and make an informed choice rather than stumbling into what can end up feeling like a chore.

Schedule Me Time

One last self-care strategy that even I don't do enough of is schedule me time. This literally means picking a couple of days out of the month and scheduling yourself into your calendar. For instance, on those days that I have handpicked for myself I decline invites, I decline appointments, and I remove myself from social media. I consider myself busy, dedicating that time to myself. This is important because we get so wrapped up in our commitments that we forget about ourselves. We end up having calendars full of obligations in the form or appointments and deadlines and we wonder why we are so stressed.

You have to realize that it's necessary to schedule time for self. Pick a day and decide that on that day it will be all about you. You won't be bothered with emails, events, projects, etc. Instead you will focus on restoring your peace and clarity. This will give you the chance to recharge so that when you go back to being booked and busy you can be the superwoman that you were meant to be.

Create Boundaries with No Apology

As women we were created to set a precedent of excellence; however, I don't think that included us running ourselves ragged to do so. Despite our natural instincts to be nurturers and supporters it was never intended for us to get lost in those roles because our greatness extends beyond them. We are women of resource but that resource will go without being utilized if we don't create balance in our lives. In knowing this we should strive to be aware of our commitments and embrace the idea of setting boundaries.

Setting boundaries ultimately means understanding your personal limits and protecting your peace. It requires that you create space for personal growth by limiting unwanted and often unnecessary interference from the outside world. It's being mindful of your commitments and choosing where to draw the line. This means no more overcommitting or giving beyond what's available. If this is not understood by others it's not your job to explain; sorry, not sorry!

Don't feel guilty for choosing to view yourself as important. Don't apologize for creating boundaries and prioritizing yourself. If anything, understand that it is your personal responsibility to make sure you're taken care of. You have to learn to nurture the woman you are in order to excel as the woman you desire to be.

Chapter Six

Gold Digger

How to Mind and Mine Your Own Business
Lakichay Nadira Muhammad

Once you have decided to own your own business or pursue the profession that makes you sing, then it should be easy breezy to move forth doing what you are destined to do, right? Well, not so fast. I am sure as business owners and career professionals, we all have a story where we may have had a few challenges along the way. Let's face it, the path to owning a business or working in a profession that we have chosen is not always what others may make it out to be. First, we must make sure that our focus is in the right place and on the right thing. It can be so easy to get caught up with everything that is going on around us, even when everything that is going on around us has absolutely nothing to do with us. This is why I believe that one key ingredient to being successful when it comes to "minding our business" is to make sure that we remain focused.

Haven't you noticed that distractions seem to be everywhere, especially when we decide that we want to focus on a particular goal? I know for me, I have had an army of distractions that seem like they always want to show up when I am attempting to be razor focused. Take for example when I started working on this book. It seemed like everybody on the planet needed my attention. I mean, it was a struggle to just sit in one place for a set amount of time because life and people were calling my name, and boy was my name being called LOUDLY. Every single time that I made any attempt to sit down and focus on this very important task, there seemed to be some kind of crisis, person, or situation that appeared to need me more than the one I was attempting to focus on. In many cases I completely submitted to the call, even when it didn't concern me, even when what tugged at me didn't have a darn thing to do with me. Yep, I was guilty as charged. I was caught red-handed. I realized that I too had gotten caught up minding someone else's business at the risk of abandoning my own.

Minding other folks' business can be an easy thing to do, so if you just happen to have fallen victim once upon a time, or if you are currently operating as the head of the nosy department, don't beat yourself up too badly. There is still an opportunity to break free! Take it from somebody who has been there and done that on a multitude of occasions. One thing that I have learned is that minding other folk's business is a risky behavior, as it can cost you far more than you are willing to pay and often much more than what it is worth.

There can be many indicators that can help us to determine what minding someone else's business could possibly look like. Let's look at a few of these areas just so that we can see if any of them hits home and needs to be addressed or possibly adjusted in our own front yard. As we take a look at these indicators, let's also look in the mirror, be honest, and ask if any of these apply to us or is it just a close coincidence.

1. **Distractions**

Earlier, I spoke on how easy it was for me to get distracted. Sometimes we are caught up in other folks' business by way of being distracted. Basically, you were attempting to focus on your own business and before you knew it you were pulled in to deal with something that was unrelated to your focus, either willingly or unwillingly. A distraction can be anything that prevents someone from giving full attention to something else. Some synonyms of a distraction are diversion, interruption, disturbance, intrusion, interference, obstruction, and hindrance.

2. **Nosy**

Yep, I said it. I mean somebody had to. Seriously, we all may be guilty of being a little nosy. A perfect case of being nosy is when other people have something going on and we deliberately seek out information or concern ourselves with what they are doing. Bottom line, it's not our business and we go seeking to gain more information that doesn't serve us professionally or towards the betterment of our business. When a person is being nosy that means that they are showing too much curiosity about other people's affairs. Some synonyms for nosy are prying, inquisitive, curious, busybody, probing, spying, eavesdropping, and intrusive.

3. Unsolicited advice

Unsolicited advice is when you tell other people what you think is best based on your professional opinion or experience and that opinion was not requested. Often when we are an expert or have an experience in a particular area it is super easy to get tangled into this one. Naturally we desire to give a helping hand or "fix things" if we can, but this can sometimes land us in trouble. I must admit that this one hit home like a ton of bricks for me. As a therapist and a holistic health practitioner, I have found myself deep down the rabbit hole of offering unsolicited advice time and time again. Always having a desire to "help" others "fix" their challenges has fueled me in the past to jump in like Superwoman to the rescue. Although when I first started exercising the art of minding my business it was difficult to control my urge to want to just jump right in and come to the rescue of others, but since I have been in "recovery" it has been most rewarding to see that I am slowly but surely getting better and better each day. Offering unsolicited advice can be both expensive and exhausting. Synonyms include uninvited, unsought, unasked for, unrequested, uncalled for, unwelcome, spontaneous, and voluntary.

For the record, I want to be clear on my stance with offering unsolicited advice. I am not saying that this can NEVER be done, I am just strongly suggesting that before we jump in and put that cape on to offer our advice, we need to make sure that we have done our due diligence on the matter at hand. Helping others when they are in need is a beautiful thing that the world needs to see more of. However, there is an extra thin line that we need to take notice of before we offer up advice that no one asked us for.

4. **Meddling**

Often as professionals we can find ourselves wandering when we go and concern ourselves in another separate operation, department, or business that is not in alignment with our own. For example, perhaps you are the Director of Finance at Mind Your Business, INC and you find yourself worried about what's going on in the Human Resource Department. You even go so far as to impose by telling them who you think they should select to hire and by giving them additional suggestions on interviewing techniques. Now don't get me wrong or misunderstand what I am speaking of. Many of us are multitalented and may have more than one profession or more than one business venture. For those of us who are serial entrepreneurs, this doesn't always apply to us but be careful because there is still a thin line. As long as you are *clear* as to what your job description is and you stay to task, all things will be fine. However, it is important that we walk this tightrope carefully because one false move can have us turned upside down. Synonyms for meddle include interfere, butt in, intrude, pry, poke, interpose, busybody.

You might wonder why I provided synonyms after each description of the indicators. I intentionally took an extra step to provide these synonyms, because sometimes when we are going through a process of self-evaluation and self-correction we will make excuses to not be honest or to take a closer look to see if we are a match to the things that may describe our behavior. Sometimes we may need an additional mirror or two to make sure that we can see the whole cute or ugly picture.

We can go on and on to talk about additional ways that we can find ourselves minding other people's business, but I only wanted to touch on a few. I believe there are enough mentioned here to get a good understanding of my point. It is critical that whether we are working within our desired career or building, or developing and growing a business, that we keep focused on what matters the most. We cannot be fully successful if we don't put the necessary care into our OWN Business.

Speaking of OWN, think about Oprah's OWN Network. Forbes estimated that Oprah's share of OWN is worth about $75 million dollars. Do we think that this could even be possible if Oprah was minding the business of Lifetime, CSPAN, PBS, or any other networks? Absolutely not! This however is not to say that she did not research these other companies to learn about the trends and any other information that was necessary to establish her business. It simply means that she understood that in order for her to get to the TOP of her game as a businesswoman, she would have to nurture and *mind her own business.* Oprah is a perfect example to use for this type of subject matter. Oprah, as many may agree, is one of the most influential and successful business women in this country. For those of us who have multiple businesses and are multitalented, Oprah is an excellent example of how you can take your multiple gifts and talents and merge them together to create a masterpiece that has the potential to turn into your very own empire. The key to it all is learning to mind YOUR OWN business!

I once read a Facebook meme that read "How to be Successful: Mind your own Business." It tickled me, probably because these few words spoke a mountain of wisdom. The operative word in the meme was SUCCESSFUL. As business owners and professionals who are working in their career choice, I would like to think that one of our goals is to obtain a level of success. I mean, why be in business or choose a specific profession if we don't desire success? By now I am sure that we all have some definition of what we consider to be success. I look at success as a personal mark of achievement that looks different for all us. Success for one person could be to obtain the highest educational degree within their field. Success for someone else could mean being in a position where they can pull others up the ladder of an industry. No matter how we define success for ourselves, it still requires focus and concentration of a specific goal. Therefore, the meme earlier made so much sense. I mean what does it profit a woman to gain her wings and soar to the top only to turn around and lose her heightened status because she chose to spend too much time minding someone else's business and not enough time minding her own?

Luke 6:42 reads, "How can you say to your brother, 'Brother, let me take out the speck that is in your eye,' when you yourself do not see the log that is in your own eye? You hypocrite, first take the log out of your own eye, and then you will see clearly to take out the speck that is in your brother's eye."

Mining

When someone mentions the word mining what automatically comes to your mind? Do you think of men in hats with an affixed flashlight and a pair of steel toe boots? For years this is the very thing that would come to my mind when I heard the word mining. Mining has a few different definitions. Webster's dictionary defines mining as follows:

1. to dig in the earth for the purpose of extracting ores, coal, etc.;

2. to avail oneself of or draw useful or valuable material from.

3. an abundant source.

Each of these definitions has significant meaning as it relates to the human being and our human potential.

There are many things that one may choose to mine. Whether one delights in gold, copper, iron, diamonds, coal, silver, or uranium, all are precious materials from the richness of the earth. All require a different technique, method, and process to extract. One of the things that is interesting about the mining endeavor is that it changes depending on what you choose to mine. Some of the earth's riches require surface mining where other materials may require underground or sub- mining. When looking at the comprehensive steps and stages in the process that we know as mining, I find it intriguing that there is such a myriad of steps and stages depending on what you choose to focus on. What fascinates me the most is the correlation between mining minerals of the earth and mining and extracting the best within ourselves and our business.

When I look at the parallels between ourselves and our business, I see them as being one in the same. We ultimately make up "our business". Without our intelligence and knowledge, we could never be successful in any profession or career choice. Therefore, when I think about what it means to "mine your business" I look at it through a "wholistic" set of lenses. In my practice as a "wholistic" versus holistic practitioner, I help my clients to obtain optimal health and wellness by digging deep and helping them to align themselves mentally, physically, spiritually, and emotionally. All four of these components make up the WHOLE person, leaving no "holes" in their treatment. As we "mine our business" it is equally important for us to examine every aspect of ourselves and our business. For clarity, when I say business I am referring to our actual business if we are business owners or the business that we tend to within the organization or company that we invested our time and energy in also known as our professional career.

To "mine our business" means that we must engage in a process that will drive us to dig deep into the hearts and the minds of who we are and the various qualities and characteristics that make us unique and ultimately make us great. The other part of that is to use the same method to dig deep into the unique characteristics of what helps our business stand out and sets us apart from other professions and businesses.

There is a distinctive and critical process to what it must take for us to be "properly mined". I believe that if we are going to be successful leaders, business owners, and professionals of any kind, it would do us well if we were deliberately mining our business and making sure that we are equipped with all the proper tools before we even began the process.

As business owners, entrepreneurs, and talented and gifted professionals we must respect and appreciate the mining process in its totality. It is far too easy and much more comfortable to not want to fully accept all aspects of the mining process. However, I am sure that we agree that in order for us to extract the absolute best from ourselves and our business, we must fully be available and ready to roll up our sleeves to enter into the mine and begin "mining our own business". Similarly, when we are focused on "minding our business", "mining our business" can equally require discipline, sacrifice, and the ability to stay focused.

Additionally, mining our business forces us to dig just a little deeper. Below are just a few basics things that we may want to consider. These are tools that will aid any business owner or career professional to maximize the activity that goes into their personal mining process.

1. Knowing your Value

As we embark on the journey of "mining our business" it is important that we have a clear understanding of who we are and the talents and the gifts that we bring to the table. I believe that for every talent and gift that we see or know that we have, there are many more of those gifts and talents that are buried deep within us that we don't see and may not even be aware of. The mining process requires that the person doing the mining be on the lookout for anything that appears to be of value. As a miner you must have a keen ability to recognize the good from the bad and the valuable from those things that may not be as valuable. When you think about your current position or career choice or about the business that you decided to open, what is the one thing of value that sets you and your business apart from all the rest of the people and businesses that may be similar? This is an important question because this will help you to determine how valuable your talents and services can be to the market that you serve. For example, if you work for a hospital and you are the only staff member that has a particular type of training that the hospital needs, the value that you add and bring to the table is the unique training that you have. This could possibly mean that the hospital may pay you a higher salary based on the value that you bring to the table.

I remember working as a contractor for a private home health agency where I was the only social worker amongst a team of other professionals. The company had multiple nurses, a few occupational and physical therapists, speech therapists, and a handful of doctors. Due to me being the only social worker on staff, I was able to negotiate a higher contract and I was called upon more often. When different issues came up that required my expertise, I was the one that the company depended on. Additionally, for the company to stay in compliance, they had to have a social worker on board. I was able bring that skill set to the table and add value. Knowing my value gave me a greater edge and opened up room for negotiation and leverage. At the end of the day, know what makes you, or your product or service unique and always market those benefits. Your knowledge of your value is one of the greatest assets outside of your talent and gift.

2. Nurturing the seed

Every good farmer knows that one of the key ways to ensure that their crop is going to be fruitful is to make sure that the seeds that have been planted are given everything that they need. The nurturing process requires that you first ensure that the precious seed has been planted in good fertile soil. Also, there are certain natural resources such as the right land, certain nutrients, and the right amount of water, sunlight, and air are also present. The farmer also has to make sure that he/she is able to physically provide the energy that is necessary to work the land. As a farmer, you need to nurture your crop from germination to harvest. Some of the same requirements that are needed for a good farmer are very similar to the requirements that are needed for those of us who seek to mine our business. All of the talents and gifts that we have must be properly nurtured and they must have the right conditions in order to develop and grow. Our talents and gifts in their infant state need a lot of TLC in order that they manifest into a well-developed work of art, a masterpiece. Just like the farmer who desires the growth of his seeds we too are farmers in our garden, aka "gold mine". The farmer sees the potential and honors and respects the universal principles for growth. We must honor and respect the same principles. Underneath the darkness of the dirt and buried deep is a seed that is waiting to be harvested. Deep within any mine are rich resources that can only come forth by the proper extraction. As we mine our business we should eventually take on the spirit of the farmer. If the farmer gave up and abandoned his farm, he could ultimately interrupt the growth of his harvest. If the farmer got tired and decided that the work was to laborious, there would be many people who wouldn't be able to reap the benefits of the bountiful harvest that could have come from the farmers hard work. Our talents and gifts are like the seeds of the farmer. Just like the farmer we need to nurture our crop from germination to harvest.

3. Come equipped

Now let's first look at the tools that it takes for one to be able to properly mine resources and extract the abundant source. We must make sure that the tools that we use to mine are a good match for what we are mining. For example, mining gold is quite different from mining copper, diamonds, platinum, and silver. Not only are the tools different but the process is different as well. If we were on our way to play or participate in our favorite sport or activity we would make sure that we were dressed appropriately. If I knew that I was on my way swimming at the beach or to play basketball it would be ridiculous and irresponsible for me to show up with my Sunday's best on. Making sure that we have the proper tools that we need to handle the job is a must in any business or profession. How can we properly get the job done if we are lacking the very things that we need to keep the wheels rolling? Not coming equipped will never get us the best results. This also requires that we are clear as to what the job is that we are getting ready to embark upon. I remember once having a plumber come out for a house call. When I explained to the plumber what I thought was the problem he bought the equipment that he assumed that he would need. Well, because I really was only able to give him information that came from a limited view of my understanding of the matter he made a decision that ultimately cost him a second and third trip to my home, because he did not come equipped. What type of tools and equipment do you need to make your business successful? Is there a specific training or education that you can use that will help you to do your job even better? Ultimately, we are not able to fully get the job done in the best way if we don't have all that we need. When we lack information and knowledge, tools, or other important and necessary equipment, we can set ourselves up to fail and make unnecessary mistakes.

4. Investing in the best for the best

We have all heard the saying that the best deserves the best. As business owners and business professionals it is important that we are always pouring into ourselves giving ourselves the best that this world has to offer us. If we expect to get the best from our mining process, we must make sure that our actions are in alignment with our expectations. Our brand-new Jaguar is not going to do well running on 87 octanes, just like our precious bodies will not be able to handle a diet built on junk food. Our businesses, our gifts, and our talents are equally deserving of the very best. Feeding and providing our business and ourselves with the best will ensure that we are equally able to produce the best.

As I have studied the complexities of the mining process, the things that stand out the most is having a thorough knowledge of the work that you are undertaking, having the right tools, accepting that there are multiple methods of mining, and understanding that there are many stages as well. Did you know that on average, it takes between 10-20 and in some cases 30 years before a gold mine is even ready to produce material that can be refined? Yes, 10, 20, and 30 years. There is a lot to be said here, especially as it relates to us mining our business. It is a reminder that it takes time for our gifts and talents to grow. Knowing that the process doesn't happen overnight allows for what is being mined to experience the proper nurturing, growth, and specialized development. Time, just like our own sacred gifts and talents, is a valuable commodity.

When digging for gold, one must be focused and deliberately moving in a direction, operating from a high expectation, knowing that as you dig you are on a journey of digging for the purest and most valuable resource. Our dig is great because what we are digging for is even greater. Let us continue to mind our business so that we will be champions at mining our business. The reality is that when we are focused on doing what we should be doing and when we are doing it to the absolute best of our abilities, we will find that we don't have much time left to mind anyone's business but our own.

Chapter Seven
Self-care in the Process of Change

Krystal Humphrey

"When we self-regulate well, we are better able to control the trajectory of our emotional lives and resulting actions based on our values and sense of purpose."– Amy Leigh Mercree

Change is one of the undeniable absolutes that will be met many times throughout the process of living. It can be one of the most beautiful and liberating experiences if we are open to it without undue resistance caused by fear. During these shifting periods, we can encounter episodes of uncertainty and even duress. Naturally, we are inclined to do all that we can with our resources, such as intellect, the sphere of our network, time, gifts and talents, to moderate the impact of change.

Successful navigation through all our changes, whether intentional or prescribed by life, comes with the mandate of self-care. For many people, including myself at various periods in life, self-care is hardly a thought much less a priority. Instead, aspirations for career and family, for example, can disproportionately usurp the attention that we need to gift to ourselves. That is not to say that reaching established goals are not important. However, the idea is to affirm ourselves as a priority so that we can nurture all of the components of the self.

I began my professional counseling private practice in 2014 without so much as having ever attended a business class, let alone being equipped with business basics. I can admit now that it was a bit of arrogance that made me leap when I was not necessarily prepared. Nonetheless, I pursued in my new lane with all the passion that I could give because it was, of course, my greatest asset at the time. It was inconceivable that I would fail at making an everlasting impression on the lives of those who would find themselves sitting on my couch. I was adorned with my "healing cape" ready to save the world. I found myself digging so intentionally into this unchartered territory that before I knew it, I had forgotten to breathe. I had forfeited balance so that I could prove to "them" that they were right to cheer for me. In essence, I thrived on outward validation since I had not created space in all of my business to do that for myself. Consequentially, my lack of self-care nearly forced me back to the shores when all I wanted to do was swim in the deep. I became the counselor who needed a counselor given that I did not refuel effectively once I emptied of myself. Change had come but I did not handle it gracefully. It was then that I realized that my own mental, emotional, physical, and spiritual health had to be factored into all my pursuits. As I reflect, I am thoughtful of the many lessons concerning mental self-care learned in this experience.

No...What a powerful word! Once upon a time I was one in the population of people who always has a "yes" in her spirit. Unfortunately, it was not necessarily in response to God. For years, I conducted my life under the false pretense that people needed me to say yes because I could be their saving grace. What pride! Often I was affirmative when the benefit for me, and perhaps them too, was in the decline. Anger began to be a regular condition of my heart the more frequently I opposed myself, disregarding my own needs. An appropriately placed and timely "no" is necessary for the sake of protecting your inner peace, especially while experiencing transitions in your life. I am happy to know that I am not responsible for anyone's feelings except my own. We ought to be considerate of the potential influence we have over other feelings based upon our actions, but do not have to oblige ourselves in carrying the weight of resolving those feelings for them.

I began to understand that I was not kind nor patient enough with myself while I was learning about the world of business while also discovering a new level of personal fortitude. This created doubt and frustration as I held firmly to unrealistic expectations of myself when I first ventured into entrepreneurship. Instead of allowing the removal of my "comfort zone" to strengthen me, it frightened me as I am sure it does for many others. For those of us who believe that there is a script that details how we *should* feel, think, or do during change, my message is to let it go; just be. Give yourself permission to not know all the answers. Give yourself permission to be vulnerable. Give yourself permission to feel, think, and do without expectation of perfection. In doing so, you create more space for healthy, emotional development.

Self-care is an all-encompassing concept with many facets and considerations. Ultimately, it is making yourself a priority no matter what is happening in your life including all your transitions. Just say "no" and give yourself permission to love who, where, and what you are!

Chapter Eight
State of Mind
Journaling into a Greater Self-efficacy
Gigi Brown

If we are not intentional and clear on what we want in life, it's easy to find ourselves somewhere that doesn't feel good to our soul. I was in my late 40's when I found myself in a place that did not feel good to my soul. I was filled with discontentment and had begun to accept that where I was in my present life had everything to do with my own decisions.

I had dropped out of college during the 1980's. It had always bothered me that I did not complete my degree. Year after year I promised myself that I would return to school. The years went by and I still did not have my degree. I was making promises to myself that were not backed by intentional action. It would be 26 years later, at the age of 48 that I would finally walk across the stage and receive my degree.

When I finally began to do the work to figure out why I was so angry and frustrated with my life, I discovered that the intentions that I verbalized were not consistently met with follow through. There was a gap between what I professed to want, to value, and what I was getting in life. I began to realize that I wasn't happy with me. This realization didn't happen immediately; I didn't immediately realize I was the problem. No; I thought it was my job, my relationship, my friendships…anything and everything but me.

I returned to complete my undergraduate degree thinking it would help me get a better job and that it would lead to more happiness. While working full-time, I enrolled in college full-time. I hadn't been in an institution of higher learning in 25 plus years. It would be an understatement to say that it was challenging. I wasn't prepared for the advancement in technology, nor had I ever taken an online class before. I was anxious, afraid of failing, lacking in confidence, but excited. My excitement to be actively doing something that I felt would help move me closer to a place of happiness, maybe even joy, is what pushed me past my nervousness and fearfulness.

When I reflect on that time in my life, I think it is when I began to truly realize that when there is a desire that is stronger than my fear, my anxiety, and my lack of confidence, I make a move. I take action. It is safe to say that when the desire is strong enough, it will move you pass your fear, anxiety, and lack of confidence. I realized this, and it is exactly what I did. I moved into action.

After years of not journaling, I began to journal again, I started back journaling a year or so before I returned to school to complete my undergraduate degree. I wrote down my goals. This was something else I hadn't done in years. That first year back in school, I was introduced to goal setting. I became familiar with "SMART" goals. These are goals that are specific, measurable, achievable, realistic, and timely. I was learning, and my excitement grew. Where I once went into work dragging, reluctant, and ungrateful; I began to go to work smiling, energetic, and grateful. This led me to a second realization…the pursuit of something that matters to a person changes their perspective.

The excitement and opportunities to learn gave me a different perspective concerning myself and my job. I was putting in the time to follow one of my passions--obtaining my degree and learning.

I became fascinated with goal setting. I set a goal to journal daily. After not having journaled in years, this goal didn't happen overnight. I had to work and work at this goal. There are still times, I will miss days in my journaling, but I always return to it. The days between my last entries have become less and less. All goals are not created equal. Some goals take more discipline and time to become a habit. I discovered that when I accomplished a goal that required more discipline and more of my time that this usually was a direct indication of how strongly I desired that goal.

One of the beautiful things about setting goals and journaling about them is that you can't hide from your progress on your goals. If I lost my focus, I only needed to consult the entries in my journal to remind myself of what I wrote down as my intentions.

I completed my undergraduate degree without much of a problem. After I completed the degree, I remained at the same company and began once again feeling frustrated, unfulfilled, and stuck. I did receive a promotion, but it was in the same department, doing the same work. The only difference was I was the only manager in my sub-department now. The company had survived bankruptcy and downsized its workforce. I was excited to be in a role that gave me the opportunity to grow and make more decisions. At least that's what I thought at that time. When I reflect, I realize I settled. I had gone back to school to get my degree to gain additional skills and to be more marketable. Yet, I was at the same company. When I really thought about it, I was promoted into a role that I didn't really want. It was a role that I settled for.

Why? Why was I settling? At the time, I wasn't ready to learn the truth about why I was settling. So, what did I do? I went back to school to get my master's. After reading through my journal, I realized that I had set getting my master's as a goal. I looked at the other goals I had written down and thought wow these are some huge goals. My journal pointed out to me what I wanted…what I was too afraid to admit other than on the lines of my journal. For instance, my journaling revealed that I wanted my college degree because education was important to me…so important that I did not feel good about myself without the degree.

I began to journal more and more and realized that my journal gave me a way to check in on my integrity with myself. Was I being honest about what I wanted in life? Were my values my own or set by my upbringing and society? Was I settling because I didn't feel worthy or good enough? And the biggest question of all…what did I see myself doing that made me excited and placed me into a state of joy just thinking about doing it? I didn't immediately know the answer to this question. I did somehow know that if I continued to journal; I would find more and more out about who I was really was. Thus, I continued journaling and setting goals.

After a couple of years of being out of school and feeling incomplete still, I went back to school again, this time to get my Masters. I was slightly over 50 by now. I had friends and acquaintances ask why I wanted to go back to school at my age. They didn't understand it and where I would have previously felt uncomfortable and unsure about my decision based on another's opinion, I felt calm and assured. I was making progress in my self-confidence and faith in myself. The opinions of others were ceasing to have the impact that they once had. Why? I discovered that setting goals and accomplishing them is a confidence booster.

I refused to give space to any negative thoughts that I was feeling about returning to school. I was learning the importance of eliminating all thoughts that did not support my greater good. I moved past the fear, applied to a school I admired, and I was accepted. The writing was intensive as was the research. Yet, I would not change my decision today about joining the master's program at Mercer University. I learned even more about myself during the program. I learned that I was a serious procrastinator, but that wasn't really a surprise. It was more surprising to finally acknowledge this about me, to myself. I know it may sound crazy, but so often it is the lies that we tell ourselves that keep us stuck. I certainly had a suitcase of lies to unpack about me.

Moving forward past the self-doubt, my changes made a big impact on how I thought of myself. In the first class of my master's program I had a professor that required us to keep a journal as we read Parker Palmer's, "Let Your Life Speak." That class, that professor, that book, and my journaling helped me change my "state of mind." I realized that I hadn't thought of myself in the most positive light. I realized during the master's program, that I was unhappy in my life because I was playing small. I was not going after what resonated with my spirit. I was remaining at a job where I was no longer growing. I was doing work that I was not passionate about. I was allowing fear to immobilize me.

That semester I filled up a complete journal of over 100 pages with my thoughts. Those blank pages of my journal that I began to fill up with my greatest desires and my deepest pains helped me move into action. I moved into action to take control of my life. I wrote away my fear, my self-doubt, my anger, my feelings of inadequacy, and all the lies that I had told myself about what I couldn't do or couldn't have. I journaled my way into self-efficacy. I began to see myself in a different, kinder, more loving way. As I began to see my skills and my natural gifts in a new light, I also began to see myself doing what I enjoyed-- writing, researching, conducting one-on-one interviews, engaging in public speaking, and encouraging others to reconnect with the desires of their heart. Changing my state of mind began to completely change my life. I began to make and set goals, make decisions, and have results that resonated with my soul. I began to live a life that I was happy with and that I knew I came into this world to have.

It's such a revealing experience anytime I go back and read what I've written in my journal. When I read my thoughts and my intentions, I come face to face with me. I admit I have cried a few times when I read how far I've come in so many areas of my life. I also laugh at myself in such a good way when I read the thoughts of a woman that is now moving in unison with her spirit. I now have many journals that are filled with my thoughts. I have journaled myself into a self-efficacy that says I can do anything that I am willing to put the time and work into.

Journaling is one of the most powerful, under-used tools to help one change their life. My journal has helped move me from a subconsciousness of not being enough and of not being worthy to a consciousness of knowing that I am incredibly and magnificently created to do great work. If I could, I would gift every person with a journal and provide only one request--just write something every single day. May you journal your way into a self-efficacy that allows you to fulfill your greatest desires.

Chapter Nine

Unwrapped Gifts: Tapping into the Divine Power Within

A Journey of Self-discovery

Lakichay Nadira Muhammad

"We each are gifted in our own unique and special way. It is our duty to discover our own special light. Discovering that light within yourself can serve as a beautiful light and gift to someone else." **Lakichay Nadirah**

A gift is a word that has several different meanings and therefore can be used in a variety of ways. Merriam Webster describes a gift in the following way:

noun

1.: a notable capacity, talent or endowment

2.: something voluntarily transferred by one person to another without compensation

3.: the act, right, or power of giving

verb

1.: to endow with some power quality, or attribute

2.: a present

Have you ever been given a gift of any kind? I'm sure that you may be thinking, what a silly question, right? Of course, you have. We all have been given gifts within our lifetime. Some of us have been blessed to have received a multitude of gifts. Usually when a person gives a gift, they are giving it to us because they care for us and want to show some form of appreciation towards. In some cases, gift giving is an opportunity to express one's love for us. When a person truly cares for the person that they are giving a gift to, they are very particular and may be very selective about the type of gift that they choose. They want to ensure that the person that they are giving this gift to can benefit from the gift and the gift is in alignment with who they are.

Imagine if you were the person on the giving end and you decided that you wanted to gift someone with something uniquely special. You took your time to choose and select the "perfect gift". Now imagine how you might feel, if after giving this special hand-picked gift, you asked the person who you had given this gift to did you like it" "What did you think of the gift?" They then responded by saying, "Oh, I haven't had an opportunity to open your gift," or "The gift is nice but I haven't had the opportunity to use it yet. I'm sure I will get around to using it later." How would this response make you feel? How would you feel knowing that you spent precious time and energy preparing or choosing something extra special to give to someone who hasn't even opened or made use of the special gift that you selected especially for them?

Let's take a closer look at another type of gift. Of course, we have gifts that may be given to us by friends and families, but what about gifts that we have been endowed with, like the gift that is unique to you, your special attribute? You know, that gift that others can benefit from? For example, some people have been gifted with the ability speak very well. Others have been gifted with the ability to heal or sing, build, inspire, and motivate other people. I could sound off an endless list, but the point is we all have something very special within. Some of us may know what our gifts are, and some may not. In many cases we can often look at others and can clearly see what they may be good at and what brings them happiness.

When reflecting on the intangible, immaterial, or more spiritual gifts, have you been given any gifts that still remain in the package? If you can honestly answer this question with a no, I salute you. I offer the original salute, a smile. From my experiences, both personally and professionally, I have seen many people with many gifts and talents that go unwrapped, unused, and unopened. What a shame! The one thing that is a fact is that no gift that could ever be of any benefit to anyone if it remains unopened, unused, or unwrapped.

Our gift is our power source; it is like our weapon that can be used to change the world or like a superpower. The reason cartoons and movies depicting superheroes intrigue us is because deep down inside we are reminded of ourselves. Innately we can relate and we long to emulate what we see on the big screen in our own everyday reality.

Each one of us has a gift, but unfortunately, many of us will die with our gifts buried in our soul. Our gifts were never meant to lay dormant; our gifts were meant to come alive, to transform into action. We must fight to keep and strive to use the gifts that we have been given. The gift is our divine birthright; therefore, it should be our divine life fight to make sure that we make use of it by any means necessary.

What happens when a package is sent through the post office and the package has been specially delivered and requires a signature to receive it? What if the person on the receiving end chooses not to sign for the gift or disregards the notices stating that there is a package waiting to be picked up? In most cases the package is returned to the sender, right? Well what would happen if our divine gifts were also returned to the sender when we chose not to open, sign for, or take notice of them? If our divine gifts were to be returned to the sender, it would have to be returned to the one who is responsible for giving the gifts. In this case it would be returned to The Chief Gift Giver, The Creator and Author of all gifts; the very one who has given us life. If the gift giver is merciful enough to give us a divine gift and we make the choice not to open it, couldn't this act be considered an act of ingratitude? One of the definitions of ingratitude is the lack of appreciation or thanks for something received, and the lack of thankfulness. I would, therefore, say absolutely.

I think it is fair to say that we can never accuse the Chief Gift Giver of not having the right address or making a mistake as to where to deliver our spiritually divine gifts. Unlike many of the tangible gifts that we may have received in past times, our divine gifts will always end up in the right place. The question becomes, will the receiver of the gift receive the gift and do with it what is destined? When we were gifted with the breath of life, when we were gifted with that germinating seed of the most powerful life force, when your mothers egg met with the sperm of your father and the two came together to become one which ultimately created you, this was indeed one of your divine gifts.

I spent many years studying and perfecting my gifts. I am blessed like most of you to have been given a couple of gifts. As a Wholistic Health Practitioner, I am intuitive about healing. Often, I can close my eyes, tune in to my clients and determine what they need based on what I see and the energy that I feel. I've been this way for years. I also have a gift for being able to read the energy and see the colors associated with individuals. Even I didn't always accept my gifts. I recognize there were many times where I ignored them. As an empath, I often find myself caught up into the feelings of others, concerned deeply with how others feel or have a strong desire to rescue people from internal and external pain. It took me years to really understand my purpose in life. I eventually recognized if I did not try identifying my gifts and learn to use them, I would never truly be satisfied and fulfilled. I also have a gift for helping others discover and tap into their own gifts. This is one of the reasons that I chose to write about my experiences and perspectives. As I begin to study what I love most about me, I was able to recognize that my "high" comes from service to others. I am divinely gifted in the healing arts. It would be fair to say that being of service to others is one of my "Love Languages". If ever I could not be of service to other's my heart would experience a deep feeling of pain. I know this to be a fact. When there is an interference or a prevention of someone's gift or talent, they will respond in a manner of which they display unhappiness or pain and discomfort. We can never truly be satisfied and complete in life until we are able to discover our gifts. The inability to discover the gift, or our life's purpose, will leave us feeling incomplete and will eventually lead to feelings of inadequacy.

It's also important to note the huge difference between recognizing your gift verses unwrapping your gift. Many will recognize that they have a gift but unwrapping one's gift requires action. Unwrapping our gifts is a process that doesn't take place overnight. For example, I can look into my PayPal account or My Square, Cash App (or whatever digital financial services that I may use for business) and notice that one of my clients/ customers has sent me a payment. If I never click to receive, deposit or transfer the payment into my account, the money will remain in limbo or cyber space. The same philosophy can be applied to our divine gifts. If we never take the time to unwrap the gifts that the Creator has so graciously bestowed upon us, then we will never reap the full benefit of the intended purpose of the divine deposit, aka gift. The process of unwrapping our divine gifts requires commitment, patience, time, appreciation, and love. It is the love that we have for the gift that will fuel the energy necessary to begin the process of unwrapping. When you unwrap something, you unveil it. You remove its covering and make known what was once hidden. Removing the veil and unwrapping our gifts is a high expression of love.

    We must treat our gifts in the most sacred of manners. Imagine if someone you loved left you an heirloom, something that had been in the family for over 100 plus years. I believe that you would go out your way to ensure the safety and protection of such a thing, especially if you understood the value of it. If we had such a prized possession, we wouldn't want any harm or damage to come to our gift because of the value that the heirloom holds. When God saw fit to give us life, He protected us in a small tight space. A space that many scientists may refer to as one of the darkest places that we will ever get the opportunity to experience, the place that we have all spent nine months or in some cases less. Yes, I am referring to that all-so-sacred womb space. It was during that time we were in constant communication with the Creator. We were in complete submission and state of obedience. The only thing we really had to do was…be. Everything else was completely orchestrated and provided for us. This was also a time that we did not need to worry about anything. All the information that we needed to know was being downloaded into our DNA. It was during this time and sacred period that our gifts were being deposited. It was during this time the Creator was most generous in our life. Maybe we didn't have a clue, but we were being formed and shaped into what we would all one day come to know as YOU.

The moment that your journey began, it was a special one. Although neither you nor your parents may have knowledge of the exact moment that you came to be, what is known is that it was indeed a moment of supreme love. Yes, Supreme LOVE. Love is a force and power that allows an activity called creation. The power and force behind love is so strong that it is responsible for each being that exists on this planet. Imagine a force so powerful that it starts with a thought, a word, and eventually becomes a full and complete being. Quite amazing. When you look at the word supreme, it is of high authority, superior to all others, it is the highest in its ranking, therefore a supreme love is the best love there can be. Supreme love was the driving energy force behind your and my creation.

I once read a scripture that stated, "In the beginning was the word, and the word was with God, and the word was God." This popular statement can be found in the first chapter and first verse the book of John. Think about this scripture and the relationship that it has with our humble beginnings.

What comes to the forefront of your mind when you read those words? Think for one moment about those powerful words. This time think about the words and close your eyes. Now imagine a time when you were housed in a space that was extremely comfortable, completely dark, and yet you felt secure. The space where creativity and the formation of great ideas all began. Let us return to that sacred space that I spoke of earlier, the womb space where we first began to feel and receive our first gift, the space that we can all say that we have spent much time. Now some of us may feel a bit weird or uncomfortable when doing this little exercise, but I challenge you to dig deep, push forward, and do it anyway. Ultimately, I wish for us all to be reminded of is the experience—the sacred interconnectedness and feeling that we all have been blessed to have. I believe that if we can be reminded of the experience, which we all know that this was once our reality, we can find a great level of appreciation and a deeper connection to our divine gifts.

Muhammad Ali once said that our service to others is the rent you pay for your room here on earth. Similarly, Shirley Chisholm once said that service is the rent we pay for the privilege of living on this earth. When I look at these two profound statements, I feel they connect to what I am sharing about our unwrapped gifts. It is our duty to incorporate the principles of gratitude as we showcase and tap in to our divine gifts. Not only is it important for us to recognize our gifts, but we must unwrap, unpackage, and use our gifts to the fullest. The use of our gifts to the fullest is a representation of the supreme love that we have been given and it will allow us to shine our bright light (gift) unto the world. This act of gratitude will allow us to live a life of fulfillment and experience complete satisfaction of knowing that we share our gifts and talents with the world and that we did not indulge in the practice of selfishness by keeping our gifts boxed up, unwrapped and unused. Our gifts and talents were never meant to be kept to ourselves but shared with the world. There is someone out there waiting on you. There is someone waiting to receive your divine gift. The question is will you begin the process of unwrapping and sharing your gift or will you hide your talents and gifts? Remember, sharing our gifts is a duty and an obligation. Very similarly to Muhammad Ali and Shirley Chisholm's philosophy, I believe that the sharing of our gifts, which come after we have recognized and unwrapped them, is the rent that we pay for the gift that we have been given by the Chief gift giver.

For those of you who have yet to recognize your gift or for those who struggle with unwrapping your gifts, I would like to present to you a challenge of love. I challenge you to set aside some time to yourself and begin to think and then write down all the things that bring you joy. Think about all the things that make you happy. Ask yourself what is it that you enjoy doing the most. If it was a job or a profession and you got paid the same amount regardless of the profession you chose, what would you want to do and why? Look closely at your answers and begin to study your personality. Think about how everything that brings you joy is in alignment with who you are. Doing these activities can help you get closer to your divine gift.

    Another thing that I would like to encourage you to do is to spend some personal time with the Creator. Spend time not only asking God but spend time listening for a response to your answer. Quiet your mind and allow yourself the freedom to receive the message or the download that contains the answers that you are seeking. I promise you that if you are sincere you will experience a revelation of what you need and the direction that you need to go in. If you tap in to the power of the divine, you will be blessed to experience your gift come to life and light.

Discovering you gift and unwrapping your gift is a beautiful experience. It is an experience that will take you on a divine journey that is sure to land you in a sacred and special space. It is my fervent prayer that if you haven't already discovered your gifts that you soon will. If, however, you have discovered your divine gifts, my prayer is that you continue to be true to your purpose, continue to unwrap your gifts, and freely share with the world.

Chapter Ten
The Call for Authentic, Servant Leaders

Gigi Brown

The visionary Civil Rights Leader, Dr. Martin Luther King, Jr. said, "Life's most persistent and urgent question is what are you doing to help others." It was a question that became very important to me later in life. I was studying leadership and had begun calling myself an Authentic, Servant leader. It sure sounded good when I would say it. It sounded good until I was asked two questions by two women leaders that I had admiration for. One of the women was a CEO of a company and the other woman was a Founder and CEO of her own worship center. I had approached each woman to ask her to participate in research I was conducting on women in the C-Suite. I was sharing with the CEO and Founder of the worship center what the research was about and what I was studying. I was asked by her during our discussion, "What have you done lately to serve others? Are you serving here at the worship center?" Those two questions should have been very easy to answer, but they proved to be difficult and then rhetorical questions as the room filled with the silence of my answers. The truth was I wasn't doing very much intentionally to serve others.

I discussed my desire to use the information from the research to create a mentoring program for women aimed at increasing the presence of women in the C-Suite with the other potential research participant. She thought the idea was good and expressed that there was a need for one, not just for women, but for men, for anyone that was interested in being mentored. I agreed, but my focus was on a mentoring program for women in the workplace. Her question to me was, "Well who are you mentoring?" I was silent for a few seconds, but I had a slightly better answer than I had with the other CEO. I was actually half mentoring one person at my place of employment. After hearing my answer, the CEO said, "Well you might want to start the question with yourself. You don't have to be a CEO, but you're in a position to mentor. Why aren't you doing more to mentor others?" Again what should have been easy questions to answer became a loud, telling silence in the room.

Those two conversations bothered me. Whenever we are bothered by something, I have learned that our feelings are trying to tell us something. We need to ask ourselves why we are bothered. I was bothered because I wasn't showing up the way I wanted to show up. I was bothered enough to sit with myself and ask myself a few questions I should have asked myself long before the conversations with the CEOs took place. I asked the questions that they asked of me and I kept sitting until I knew the answers to them. I didn't want to live a life that was not an indication of what mattered to me. Those questions from women I admired prompted me to do better and to be better.

In addition to the questions I was asked by those two women, I asked the questions below of myself:

Question one: "Who am I?" I asked myself this on a deeper level, not in terms of a role or title, i.e. mother, sister, wife, teacher, doctor, etc. To answer the question of who am I, I had to pause and become clear on what I valued and how I wanted to show up in the world. I had to spend time really digging to be sure that my values were not merely what I thought sounded good to society, but values that resonated with my spirit. I had to take the time that I had not taken years ago and get clear on who I was and how I wanted to show up. I knew that with life experiences I had changed some. I had gained more enlightenment. This enlightenment meant I needed to hold myself accountable for acting in accordance with what I valued. I made a decision to do that each day not just sometimes, but at all times. Oh, it has been work. Yet, it is work that rewards me with a gift that is immeasurable – peace.

Question two: "What problem in the world today bothers me? What problem do you feel especially concerned about?" I am sure there are several, but what are you willing to commit to serve with your time, money, or both to help eradicate? It is the persistent and urgent question that Dr. Martin Luther King, Jr. encouraged us to answer - "What are we doing to help others?"

Question three: Each evening I check in with myself to reflect on decisions I've made that day. I ask myself, "Did I make the decisions that are representative of my values? Did I listen with an open mind? What did I learn today?" Finally, I ask myself if I acted with kindness towards others.

There are many questions that we can ask of ourselves, but these are the questions and reflections that help me honor the plaque that one of my cohort members from my graduate program gave to me. That plaque simply says, "Be the change you want to see in the world."

Now if I am asked the same questions by those two women that I admire, I can fill the silence that once was with some experiences that I am passionate about and that resonate with my spirit.

If you've read this far and I still have your attention, I'd say consider what you allow to follow your "I am" statements. At work, at home, at play, wherever you find yourself, let who you are show up and be the person you say you are. The world is in need of more authentic servant leaders. I pray that you answer the call to lead and when you do, I pray that you are a D.E.E.P.P leader. A D.E.E.P.P. leader is one who continues to "develop" herself and also "develops" those that she leads, that you "empower, and "encourage" others to trust themselves and that your "passion" leads both your and others to take action. The D.E.E.P.P. leader is "passionate" about seeing those that she leads win. Her "passion" is contagious and she leads from the spirit. The D.E.E.P.P. leader "prays" for guidance and "prays" for those that she leads.

We are in need of more leaders that are self-reflective and in touch with their spiritual side. These leaders should show up at work with their spirituality with them not left at home until they turn the key in the door to return home. If each of us are clear on who we are and we take this person with us everywhere we go, we will stand for what we believe in regardless of where we are or who we are with.

It has certainly made a difference in my life. No more sitting on the sidelines when the team needs another player, someone with heart and soul to suit up and help out. No, this game of life is in need of more leaders to help create a world of wellbeing for all of humankind. The rules are simple. Know who you are, what and how you want to give back, and suit up. I've chosen the areas I'm going to commit to and if you choose your areas to commit to, we will be the change we wish to see.

Be assured that the gifts that you possess are needed. You've come into possession of this book for a reason. There are no mistakes. Honor your greatness and share it with the world. Bring your uniqueness and step forward to serve. I send you good energy and high vibrations as you step forward to help make this world a better place.

Chapter Eleven
Depression is a Real Thing

Dr. Temeca L. Richardson

Depression is a real thing.

Far too often women in business take on depression and wear it like a pair of Red Bottoms or Jimmy Choo's—we make it look good, too good at times. We send an unwavering message to the rest of the world that I'm together; I got this; this is what I do; all the while, we are broken inside. The dichotomy of the Picasso that we've constructed of ourselves to show the world juxtaposed against the millions of broken little pieces of pain that only rear their ugly little heads when we are in a quiet place, hidden from the rest of the world to see leave us in a fight that quite honestly, we cannot win.

For those of us who are in high-powered positions, or on our way, our stories seem in some ways to be the same; we are either *THE* only one, the *ONLY* one, or the only *ONE*. It's just a matter of how you identify yourself in your business. Maybe it's just you, maybe you're the top dog and you've always been that way. Maybe you're the only woman or the only woman of color at the table, or some combination of the aforementioned. The reality is, it doesn't matter because depression has a way of finding us too.

For some of us, the hard part is that we've been this strong ambitious woman for so long that we really don't know how or can't even imagine being anything else. We don't know what stress is or what it looks like until we've been under pressure for so long that our bodies just shut down on us not knowing that 'normal' people cave under the weight that we take on before the morning news has completed.

I've found in my life that God has this funny way of making us face reality. Generally speaking, we don't do a great job of listening to Him, so something has to happen to completely shut us down and believe me if you can avoid it…AVOID IT!

This kind of shut down usually comes in a big way—the loss of a job, a severe health challenge or scare, a drastic financial crisis, the loss of a loved one, or a rapid succession of many unimaginable events that no one person should bear all because we didn't listen to the subtle signs, the quiet whispers, the taps on the shoulder. The only circumstance that generally will dismantle the fortress of achievement is snatching a significant part of our foundation from under us leaving us with only one course of action: to stop. Stop going. Stop doing. Stop ignoring yourself. Stop doing for them. Stop acquiring more. Stop doing more. Just stop!

It took me many years, a serious illness, and the loss of everything before I finally came to understand how serious depression affected me as a business woman. I knew I'd had past challenges with depression, but I never really understood how severe of an affect it had on me until I was forced to stop and there was nothing left to occupy my thoughts and my mind. I didn't have to take care of others or put out fires. I wasn't taking care of my son and didn't have to worry about feeding and caring about anyone except myself. I wasn't working on overdrive and over*time* making sure the world around me wouldn't come crashing down.

During my shutdown, there was clarity in seeing how depression was affecting me. I could no longer keep how I was feeling so compartmentalized that I wasn't able to recognize the connections from my depression to my stressors at work; or from depression to the stressors in my family or to my health or any number of crosses that I was carrying all-by-myself. I had to start looking at the fact that there were a number of areas in my life that kept me from looking at, and in many respects dealing with, what was going on with my inner self.

Furthermore, it started to become very clear to me that I would wait until I was in crisis mode before I would finally ask for help. It wasn't until my depression was on me so heavy that I would *have* to deal with it. The challenge that I was able to see was that I'd be able to get immediate help for putting out an immediate fire, but I wasn't able to see the bigger picture and admit to myself that what I was experiencing (for years in many instances) was deeper than I ever cared to admit.

I was finally able to understand and admit to myself that I was really trying to uphold and maintain an *image* of success all-the-while suffering in silence. I was so focused on achieving goals, getting to the top, having a positive impact on the world, that I never stopped to take even a glimpse into seeing me. I didn't see what I was going through or what I was feeling at the time. I just kept going. And going. And going.

To be clear, I am all for us being at the top and doing what we can to change our parts of the world. However, I'm also clear that we tend to suffer in silence and won't do what is necessary to recalibrate our lives. Depression won't wait and it's one of those silent illnesses that people can't see, which often makes them unable to understand. Depression doesn't care who you are, what you have to do today, how much money you have, or how much you are needed. It doesn't take a day off or only shows up when it's convenient. If you're not careful, it can become the never-ending tunnel of darkness that winds and reconnects to itself with no way out.

We have to figure out how to get past the image of ourselves that we have for the world to see and speak from the place inside of us that recognizes how much help we really need in order to get better because better allows us to thrive. Better allows us to (re)discover our authentic selves absent of what we do in business and what we do for others. Better gives our health a chance to thrive and our spirit an opportunity to be filled. Better helps us to refocus our vision on the right now instead of always on the what's coming. Better allows us to be…us.

Lying in bed for more than 700 days had a profound effect on me in every way possible. It was during that time that I came to one simple conclusion: I wasn't going to live like that anymore. I wanted to be a different person and I wanted who I was on the inside to be just as strong as who I was portraying myself to be on the outside. I was no longer going to maintain winning and success to the outside world while existing in a profound darkness on the inside. I had to learn how to start fighting and winning more for me than I was for those who were around me.

While I am glad to know that I can win, I also realized that I cannot win alone. We cannot win alone. We have to tap into that same strength that continues to drive us in business to do the one thing that most often eludes us. That is to ask for help and to keep asking for it if we need to. Bear in mind that sometimes, the people that we *want* to help us may not be the people who *can* help us. Sometimes, they simply don't have the capacity or the complexity, or the patience, or the understanding to help us. We cannot hold them hostage or accountable for not being able to help us no matter how many sleepless nights or irreplaceable funds we gave them over the years. I've had to learn the hard way that some people just don't have the depth to help us in the places we hurt. We need to let them off the hook.

Even after taking that first step to getting help, it's imperative to understand that you may not see immediate relief from the inferno of pain that may have been building inside. You may need time off even if it seems impossible to do. You may need to be prescribed sleep aids and/or meds to help you through the tough times or even for a long time. You may need a vacation by yourself even if you stay in a room binge-watching Netflix shows while eating ice cream and ordering room service. You may need to cry…and cry…and cry.

The ultimate goal is to get *you* back. A conscious you who loves herself enough to fight through one of the darkest illnesses of all only to reemerge as the daughter that God intended for you to be. And here's the reason why…
…depression…it's a REAL thing.

Dr. Temeca L. Richardson

Chapter Twelve
The Enemy Within
Amber E. Williams

The Tell-Tale Signs

I placed one foot in front of the other begrudgingly. I managed a smile and a weak "Good Morning" to the teachers that I passed in the hallway. The wheels of my cart rumbled as it followed along behind me and my arms were full of bags, binders, and files. I stopped in front of the stairs. I hesitated and peered up the stairs. The stairs were a split flight so at least I would get a break at the landing. No elevator meant dragging this teacher cart up the stairs too. This was more than just the mid-week blues. My body made me feel like I had not gotten any rest last night, even though I went to bed exceptionally early.

I took a deep breath, lifted my cart, and placed my right foot on the first step. *That wasn't so bad*, I thought to myself. I judged too soon. By the time I got to the third step, my thigh was burning. This was the type of burning that I felt when I used to frequent the gym and worked out on the obligatory leg day. This was the same burning that usually signaled that my leg muscles had accomplished all that they could accomplish and it was time to sit down somewhere. But no such luck. I had three-fourths of a flight of stairs left and I was already out of breath. I breathed deeply, exhaled a sigh, and pressed on. My light at the end of the tunnel was the thought of sitting down when I got to my classroom.

After a week or so of experiencing pain and fatigue when climbing the stairs at work and cursing the absence of an elevator, I told my husband about what was happening. I attributed my difficulty with the stairs to weighing more than I usually do and being out of shape (I was paying 24 Hour Fitness for the opportunity to think about going to the gym). But I was slightly worried. I was used to being on the go all day long, being on my feet, and not needing a break. As a high school principal, that type of energy was a necessity. I walked hallways in heels relentlessly to make sure students were in classrooms and to monitor student behavior and teacher performance. I helped parents, welcomed district personnel, and put out whatever fires were necessary to make my school run. I spent the majority of each day on my feet. It had only been a few months since I had left my job as a principal, so I didn't understand why my body was betraying me now. My new schedule as a fifth grade teacher was less hectic and less stressful. Compared to my life just a few months ago, it was a breeze. I found myself surprised when I felt the need to rush home after each school day to take a nap. I didn't do naps. I stayed up until midnight and woke up at 5am to get things done. Napping in the middle of the day was never an option. So was I just taking advantage of the situation or was my body really winding down at 3:30pm each day? I didn't know the answer to that question but what I did know was that I could not make it through the day without a nap. My midday exhaustion got so bad that I would sneak to my car during my conference period and stretch out in the back seat to take a nap during the day. I knew something was not right.

One afternoon after school, I was feeling more drained than usual. I eliminated all plans of running errands from my mind and rushed home to get into the bed. What I felt was hard to describe—I felt malaise and fatigue, lightheaded and faint, nervous and tired, all at once. I thought that a nap would rejuvenate me, but I woke up feeling worse than when I laid down. A voice in my head told me to check my blood pressure. It took a lot of effort to locate the blood pressure monitor and measure my blood pressure. I wasn't familiar with the appropriate blood pressure measures, but the monitor indicated red so I took it as a cause for concern. I gathered myself together so I could go downstairs and tell my husband. I made it down the stairs (gingerly, at best) and found my husband sitting at the kitchen table working on some piece of machinery whose parts were strewn on the table in front of him. I sat down and began to tell him about my afternoon. After I told him my blood pressure, I got up to get a drink of water from the refrigerator. I suddenly found myself having difficulty speaking. My heart felt like it was going to jump out of my chest! My husband became alarmed and asked if I could breathe. It was difficult to, but I'm not really sure what I attempted to tell him. He brought a chair to the middle of the kitchen where I was and I collapsed into it. He informed me that he was going to call 911. I shook my head no over and over again. I didn't want to go to the hospital, and I certainly didn't want to ride in an ambulance. Either he didn't understand that I was refusing or he didn't care. He called the ambulance and they arrived swiftly. I understood everything that they were asking me but I had difficulty responding in a coherent manner. My hands and feet had a mind of their own and were repeatedly moving back and forth without my control. Other than that uncontrolled movement, I couldn't move my own muscles. I could tell that the EMTs didn't find my condition to be serious despite my elevated blood pressure and low O_2 levels—they talked to me coarsely and implied that I had control over the current situation and was choosing not to exercise it. *This is exactly why I don't want to go to the hospital*, I thought, *but no one is listening to me*. No one was listening because I couldn't speak in a coherent manner. They didn't understand what I was trying to say.

The EMTs loaded me onto the gurney and then into the ambulance. I protested the entire way. One of the EMTs rode with me in the back of the ambulance and asked me a litany of questions that I attempted to answer, but was not doing a very good job in my attempts. However, at some point I became more coherent. Becoming coherent and calming down might seem to be a good thing, but in this case, it wasn't. Despite arriving in an ambulance, my condition was no longer urgent enough to warrant immediate assistance at the ER. When I arrived, they helped me into a wheelchair and I was wheeled into the waiting room with everyone else. This was not what I wanted to do with my evening. My husband had arrived with the ambulance, so he sat in the waiting room with me. I still could not move my arms, legs, or neck, but I didn't want to be there. There was coughing, crying, and complaining in the waiting room from both adults and children and I didn't want any part of it.

Several hours passed and my name had not been called. My husband kept looking at me like he was watching for water to boil on the stove; he had a look of extreme worry on my face. I asked my husband to wheel me into a more private section of the waiting room to get away from the noise and the peering eyes. I nagged him to take me home and he refused. He was clearly far more concerned with the state of my health than I was. The longer we sat there the more my hatred for hospitals was overriding my desire to figure out what was going on with me. I bargained with him. If I get the movement back in my arms and legs, will you take me home? He agreed. At first, there was no such luck. After more time passed, I tried again and was able to slightly wiggle a toe. More time passed and I still had not been called back, but I was slowly regaining use of my limbs. I pleaded with him to take me home again and this time he agreed.

Life after my ER visit returned to normal for a while, with normal being defined as having difficulty climbing stairs and experiencing extreme fatigue. I attended work regularly and continued life as usual, with naps interjected here and there. I saw my primary care physician to get a prescription for my high blood pressure and began taking that regularly. I figured I would get better. But I was wrong.

Undeniable

One afternoon as I was wrapping up my school day, my arm began to feel weird. I was already feeling fatigued and lightheaded and I thought I would be able to finish the day and rush home for my nap. Instead, I felt a combination of pain and numbness in my left arm and I had lost the strength in my hand. I didn't want an experience at the ER like last time, but this time I was scared. I knew enough about high blood pressure and stroke to be alarmed (thanks WebMD). Right after school, I drove myself to an urgent care facility. I paid a co-pay and told them what was wrong with me. I guess my symptoms were urgent enough to jump the line because I only waited in the lobby for 2-3 minutes, then the triage nurse called me back. She took my blood pressure and it was dangerously high. I saw the doctor and he did basic tests to determine if I had suffered a stroke. He didn't feel comfortable treating me in his facility because of my history of high blood pressure so he recommended that I go to the ER and offered an ambulance ride. No ambulance for me. I drove myself to the same ER that I had visited before.

When I got to the ER, my blood pressure was high enough to warrant immediate attention this time. They moved me through triage quickly and brought me back for an EKG. After viewing the results of the EKG, the doctor was satisfied that I had not had a stroke and sent me to my own room. After waiting for quite a while (my husband had arrived in the meantime), the doctor examined me, had me perform some of the same tasks as the urgent care doctor, and ordered an x-ray of my arm and shoulder. I was discharged with pain medication, a steroid pack, and no answers. I was happy that I had not had a stroke.

Once again, I reverted to my normal routine. However, in the back of my mind, I knew my health was declining. The tingling in my hands and feet was occurring more frequently. I had to rest a lot and the stairs in my two-story home were limiting my mobility. But I am stubborn and I was not going to see a doctor anytime soon.

A close friend of my husband's passed away. We knew it was coming because we had received a phone call a couple of days before that he was in the ICU and it wasn't looking good. We visited him in the hospital and he did not look like the vibrant, resilient, humorous man that I knew. He lied in the bed connected to machines and seemed barely aware that we were present in the room. My husband chatted with him cheerily, shooting the breeze like we normally would, not really acknowledging that we were not in our living room watching TV, but were in the hospital's intensive care unit instead. We cracked jokes and talked about what we were all going to do together once he got out of the hospital. Putting up the front was hard. Seeing a strong person so vulnerable is devastating and painful. Added to that feeling was the thought that this might be the last time that we would see him. It was as if I had already started grieving.

He didn't last too long after that. We attended his funeral at a church nearby and when we arrived it was packed. By the time we walked into the church, there were only chairs for our four family members against the far wall, one in front of the other. We all sat down—my husband was first, the two boys were in the middle two chairs, and I was behind them in the rear. I hated the seating arrangement. I couldn't console my husband or properly supervise my kids, but at the same time, I wasn't feeling well and was happy to have a seat at all, especially one that allowed me to lean against the wall. I did my best to pay attention to the speaker and the program, but between my boys playing with toys that they had somehow sneaked into the church and my declining health, I was distracted. As the service progressed, I felt myself becoming weaker and weaker and more and more grateful that I was seated. I was glad that I didn't have to go to the restroom because I didn't think I would be able to make it. I sat there miserable, waiting for the service to end, with my right shoulder leaned against the wall. When it was time to go, I found it difficult to stand. I leaned heavily on the backs of chairs as we exited the church and, later, on my son. My husband wanted to socialize and, at first, I attempted to, but it became difficult to even stand. Finally, I couldn't take it anymore and asked my son to help me to make it to the car. I knew if I didn't attempt to walk to the car then, that I would have to be carried to it later.

That walk to the car was one of the longest walks of my life. I wanted to take off my heels to make the walk easier, but I knew that really wouldn't have made a difference. My feet didn't hurt. The problem was that my legs weren't working. I felt like a fawn fresh out the womb. My legs wobbled and were not sturdy. They ached and were unsteady. As I planted one foot in front of the other, I leaned most of my weight on my 11-year-old who supported me like a trooper. I kept my eyes to the ground because I felt that if I looked up, I would lose my balance. We walked in the middle of the road. I didn't care about the passing cars and how slowly I was walking. I just needed to get to the car. My son guided me to the front passenger seat and I fell into it with a plop. I waited for my husband to return.

When my husband figured out what was going on with me, he insisted that we go to the ER. I didn't want to go. After my past two experiences, I felt like it was a waste of time. I just wanted to get in my bed. But he insisted. He asked me which hospital that I wanted to go to.

"Not the one I've been going to."

We finally decided to go to the ER right outside of town. I was hoping that a change of location would bring a different result. When we arrived, I walked slowly and gingerly to the counter. After I explained what was happening, I was promptly checked in and given a wrist band. I waited in the lobby for no more than ten minutes when I was called back. I didn't know what made service more prompt this time. *Maybe I look like I'm dying,* I thought. The attendant asked us to follow him to the designated room, but I quickly realized that his request was more challenging than I realized. My pace became slower and slower. It was as if I were dragging my body along. I couldn't breathe and my whole body ached in pain. When he noticed that I couldn't keep up, he slowed down and waited. I eventually got to my assigned room, but my energy was spent and I still couldn't breathe. As I breathlessly tried to explain what was happening, my body continued to deteriorate. I was soon on oxygen. I was scheduled for a CT scan and an x-ray. Much of it was a blur, but I do remember passing out at one point when the nurse was inserting my IV. I'm not afraid of needles and I've had enough blood drawn to categorize myself as a pro. In fact, I'm the patient that likes to watch the blood being drawn. This time it was different and I felt myself about to pass out. I told the nurse, "I'm about to go," and I did. I passed out. I awoke to commotion around me. After my IV was inserted and the commotion died down, other doctors came in to survey me. I had to do more simple tasks like following the doctor's fingers, all of which I thought were easy. After my CT results and x-rays were read, the doctor was not satisfied and I was ordered to stay the night.

I can't express how adamant I was that I didn't want to stay. The only time that I had spent the night in the hospital was when I had given birth to my sons and even then I was wishing for an at-home birth. I didn't know what to expect. Hospitals were for sick people and I wasn't sick. *What about work? Who was going to take care of my kids?* I was distraught. My husband assured me that it was for the best. If I had not had insurance, I'm sure I would have gotten my wish to go home. The day after my first night there, an account manager came into the room to discuss my insurance coverage. I had not had the insurance long, nor had I reviewed the coverage for hospital stays because I never have to go to the hospital, so everything that the account manager told me was news to me. Based on his summary of my coverage, I had great insurance. It was then that they deemed it okay for me to stay there. I truly believe that if my insurance coverage would have been minimal or nonexistent, they would have found a way to release me much sooner.

I have to pause to praise the hospital that I stayed at. The room felt more like a hotel room than a hospital room (other than the rails on the bed and the constant poking me with needles). My first nurse was a young man. In the wee hours of the morning, he introduced himself to me. I think I felt an affinity for him because he reminded me of the kids that I've taught and led throughout my career. It made me happy to see him gainfully employed in a profession as a nurse, doing his job well, and exercising such a caring spirit. He sat on the couch next to me and asked me about why I was there. He didn't ask me in the way the doctors did when they wanted me to spew the facts of what happened; he asked me in a way that showed genuine concern. After listening to my story, he assured me that everything was going to be okay and that he was there for anything that I might need. When you're ill, you hear that a lot, but there was something about him that made me believe him. The other nurse that I had was a young lady who was lighthearted and humorous. Her and my male nurse got along great and you could tell that they talked about me so that they could coordinate care, especially when it came to my stubbornness about reporting pain and accepting pain medication. They both waited on me hand and foot. My phlebotomists would come in early in the morning, yet they were cheery and professional (Anyone who can draw my blood with one stick of the needle is okay with me!). I found out through talking with them that most of them worked extra shifts for the extra pay, but they were paid pretty well. The cafeteria would call me and allow me to choose my food from a menu and the delivery times. I had given up meat prior to my admittance into the hospital, but they had selections to accommodate me. I was on a restricted diet due to my high blood pressure, but the food was good.

The one thing you can be sure you will not get in a hospital is rest. Between drawing blood, checking blood pressure, and being connected to machinery, it's difficult to get rest. Initially, my condition remained the same. The doctors ran a battery of tests. At the end of the first day, I just knew that they were going to release me. I was delusional like that. My husband moved into the hospital room with me and slept on the couch which converted into something like a bed. When he was there, the nurses felt better because I was on "fall watch". If I got out of my bed without letting someone know, an alarm went off. I had to have assistance to go to the bathroom. When I was in the bed, I was on oxygen because of my difficulty breathing. I had many visitors. My family came. My friends came too. What do you really say to someone in a hospital bed? Do you talk about their illness? I'm a humorous, lighthearted person so I like to believe that I made it a little easier on my visitors, although sometimes I couldn't talk much. My friend who also happened to be my boss at the time came to visit me. She brought me gifts and sat and chatted for a while. In the beginning of those kind of visits, I felt obligated to tell my "what happened" story. Then our conversation shifted to my kids in the classroom that I had left behind and our normal girlfriend talk. Like me, she's not an outwardly emotional person. We are both stoic like that. But that day, we knew that we valued each other's friendship. One thing about hospitals is that they uncover how you really feel about people, whether for good or for bad!

It's amazing who you long for in those situations. I cried for my cousin so my husband called her and she came too. One of the hardest parts for me was informing people that I was even in the hospital in the first place. I didn't want to be there and I really didn't want people to know that I was there. Being in the hospital meant that I was weak and fallible. That wasn't me. I didn't want people to see me that way—no makeup, hair unkempt, and no bra on!

I couldn't do much protesting though and I was all the better for each visit.

My best friend (aka my sister) and her husband came to see me. They are strong in faith and I needed some of that desperately. Experiences like this make you question why it's happening. For what purpose? What will be the end result? They prayed over me and anointed me with oil from the crown of my head to the soles of my feet. When they prayed, it was the first time that I cried for myself since I had been admitted. My sister braided my hair so I would no longer look like I had endured my own personal hurricane. They sat and chatted and it was good for my emotional health.

The neurologist that was seeing me was baffled by my condition, but was very motivated to figure out what was wrong with me. I never got the opportunity to thank him for that. He suspected that I could have Myasthenia gravis; however, the test for that condition took two weeks to come back. In the interim, he prescribed me the drug used to treat it, as well as a drug to help with the nerve pain and tingling sensations. I took the medicine three times throughout the day without much optimism and spent my time watching television and chatting with my husband. That evening, I had visitors. My brother and his family came and my dad and stepmom. My room was filled with people. We always have fun when we get together and this time was no different. We joked and laughed and the nurses thought we were having a party. It wasn't until later in the visit that my husband and family pointed out that I was speaking more clearly and even moving better. I hadn't noticed until they said something. I felt happy and relieved, yet worried at the same time. That meant that the medicine was working, but that I had this condition that I had never heard of. That night, I searched on Google to find out everything I could about Myasthenia gravis. I dozed off to sleep with my phone by my side.

The next morning, I woke up and I couldn't move. I couldn't speak. My husband was snoring on the couch beside me but I could not call out to him. All I could do was lay there. I didn't understand. Last night, I was laughing and talking and this morning I was a quadriplegic. I waited for someone to come in. The attendant who took my vitals came in and saw me and ran to get the nurses. The nurses called the doctor. He determined that this was a result of overexerting myself last night and poor spacing of the timing between doses of medicine. He directed the nurse to get me another dose of the medicine and called for the speech language pathologist to come. The problem was that I couldn't swallow the medicine. I couldn't even drink water from a straw. The final plan was to grind the medicine up, mix it in a spoonful of applesauce, and see if it could go down my throat. After a few attempts, it worked.

At one point, the doctor came in to assess me and ordered a spinal tap. I lay in the bed, unable to move. The doctor stood to my left and my husband stood to my left. They were engaged in a conversation that I could not participate in. When I heard the words "spinal tap", I went into panic mode. No one was going to stick a needle in my back! When I birthed both of my children, I did so without drugs, not because I wanted to be superwoman or for some lofty ideal, but because I didn't want an epidural needle in my back! I didn't go through all that to still end up with a needle in my back! I tried to argue, but I couldn't protest the way I wanted to. For all of my efforts to speak and shake my head, I don't think my body did much. However, my tears, visibly distraught facial expression, and increasing heart rate let both the doctor and my husband know that I was vehemently opposed to this test. I would rather go home with no answers than to get a spinal tap! The doctor's answer to my distress was to give me a sedative for my anxiety. Well, it worked. I don't know what he gave me, but all became right in the world and I went through the procedure pain-free without a care in the world.

Needless to say, the spinal tap came back clear, so no answers still. Meanwhile the drug that the neurologist prescribed was working and I was regaining some of my mobility. That meant that I had regular appointments with the physical therapists. Two vibrant ladies came to my bedside with the goal of rehabilitating me. I was given bright pink putty to play with using my hands to regain my dexterity. I had to practice sitting up and getting out of bed. At first, I was insulted by these little things that they asked me to do. Of course, I could get up! I was sadly mistaken. I needed assistance to move from a sitting position to a standing position. I was devastated. I cried. This wasn't me. I had to walk with a walker and the ladies patiently walked with me as I shuffled from my hospital room to various other designations around the hospital floor. These excursions wore me out. Yet, with each passing day, I began to get a little stronger.

My final test in physical therapy was to tackle the stairwell. With the guardrail in one hand and the PT's arm in another, I was able to shuffle along on the stairs with a lot of exerted energy. I was so happy to be able to do something that, only a few months ago, I would not have even given a second thought.

I received some visitors and they noticed that I had braided my own hair. I was in good spirits and talked easily without mumbling or slurring my words. My vitals looked good. I had been weaned off of oxygen. All of that meant that it was time to go home, even though I still did not have a diagnosis. I didn't realize it at the time, but my journey was really just beginning.

Release

When I was discharged, I was sent home with a prescription for Mestinon and Gabapentin, one for my muscles and one for my nerves. I was also directed to follow up with the neurologist who had visited me briefly in the hospital. They needed to run further tests to figure out why my brain was not communicating with my muscles. I was still moving slowly and the nurse wheeled me out to the car in a wheelchair (they would have done that regardless of whether I thought I could walk or not). As happy as I was to go home, it was frustrating to have spent all of that time in the hospital and to still not have answers. The only hope was that the results for the test for Myasthenia gravis still had not come back. It wasn't that I wanted to have the condition; I just wanted an answer, even though in the back of my mind, I didn't feel like all of the symptoms fit.

Life at home was so different. My husband converted the downstairs game room into a makeshift bedroom so I wouldn't have to walk upstairs so often. I spent a lot of time resting, relaxing, and researching medical conditions on the internet. Everything seemed to point to an autoimmune disease. I just had to pick one. My mother died because of an autoimmune disease and I believed that it had been inevitable that she had passed the likelihood of developing an autoimmune illness to me.

The more I researched, the more all of the autoimmune diseases I thought I had sounded the same, except for one or two distinguishing symptoms. The Epstein-Barr virus seemed to be the catalyst for them all. I had follow-up appointments scheduled with my neurologist and rheumatologist. I had to tell my story over and over again. It was exasperating. The test for Myasthenia gravis came back negative. The neurologist conducted a nerve test on me and, after seeing that my nerves were communicating well, recommended physical therapy for my condition. I almost laughed in the doctor's face when he said this. We were sitting in an exam room and he relayed the results of my nerve test. For this visit, my dose of Mestinon was in full effect and I was moving well. The doctor asked me to cross my arms over my chest and rise from the seat in my chair. With a lot of effort, I was able to complete the task, albeit ungracefully. *How could I convey to this fool that the only reason I was able to do it was because of the medicine? Should I stop taking my medicine and then go to physical therapy? What was physical therapy to accomplish?*

When my prescriptions ran out, I was directed by the hospital to get a refill from the neurologist. They gave me a hard time. Based on my records, they didn't understand why I would be on those drugs. I had enough and broke down in tears on the telephone. Not only could they not properly diagnose me, they were refusing me the medication that gave me some semblance of normalcy. I lost it on the phone. After a tongue-lashing filled with tears and yelling, I was told that my prescription would be refilled. After all, it wasn't like I was requesting pain killers!

My rheumatologist was my best advocate. She thoroughly reviewed my hospital records and ran every test on me imaginable. Everything kept coming back negative, borderline, or inconclusive. After one especially disappointing visit when all of my tests came back negative, I was determined to find the solution myself. Armed with my Google search engine, I researched harder than I had ever searched before. I researched each of the tests that had been run on me and interpreted the results myself. I found it! At my next appointment with the rheumatologist, I was ready to tell her which test she needed to run on me next. As we debriefed in her office, she quickly mentioned that she tested me last visit for the disease that I was going to tell her about and the results were negative. I was embarrassed and devastated at the same time. I was embarrassed because I had waltzed into this doctor's office, a doctor who had worked with me diligently, and prepared to tell her what she had overlooked (although I was slightly flattered that she had and I had reached the same conclusion). I was devastated because that disease was my last hope of finding an answer. Finding an answer was necessary to find a cure. The rheumatologist recommended that I see a renowned neuromuscular specialist in the local area. I noted his name, but did not get my hopes up.

In the meantime, I had built up enough medicine in my system and developed enough strength to return to work. There was less than a month left in the school year and I didn't want to disappoint my kids. The principal, my friend, already knew that I wasn't coming back for the following year and that had nothing to do with my illness. I was honoring my one year commitment and moving on. I had decided even before my hospitalization that I would not seek full-time employment, but I would instead work from home. After so many years of working in education administration, I had missed so much time with my own children. My kids spent many evenings on school campuses and attending parent meetings with me. Add to this the constant high level of stress that I endured. I believed it was time to take a step back and devote more time to my family and to myself. Since I had become ill, I was even more committed to that decision, especially since

I was quite sure I wouldn't have the stamina for a full-time job. I was excited about being available to pick up and drop off my kids at school and spending more time at home rather than stressing at a 9 to 5 and fighting rush hour traffic every day. My ambitions were high as far as how much work I thought I could get done during the day, but I was making progress and learning what my body could and could not do. My students understood that I would not be energetically moving around the room as I normally would. Naps became my best friend and I still maintained my medication regimen. I didn't realize that those kids would be such an inspiration to me and give me so much energy. At our end of the year celebration, I was able to dance with my kids. I was so excited and encouraged!

The neurologist had given me a three-month supply because the earliest date they could schedule me for an appointment was July. As I consumed my prescription pills according to my three-times-a-day schedule, I dreading going back to the neurologist. However, the day eventually came and I had to make the trip to the doctor's office. I had my two boys with me, the drive was about thirty minutes, and I still walked at a slow, shuffling pace. I finally arrived to the doctor's office about five minutes past my appointment time. The receptionist told me that I was too late for my appointment, that I was expected to arrive fifteen minutes before my appointment time, and I would have to reschedule. Once again, I was devastated. It didn't take much these days to shatter my willpower and positive attitude. The illness had taken more than my muscle strength away. I was disappointed at the news, so I gathered my boys and shuffled out of the office to the elevator. As I got into the elevator, I became angry. As the elevator doors began to close, I blocked them with my arm. My son looked at me and asked, "What's wrong momma? Are we going home?"

"No, baby," I replied. "We're going back to the doctor's office. I burst through the glass office doors and let everything I was feeling spew out of my mouth at the receptionist. I told her about what an ordeal it was for me to travel there in my state by myself with two children in tow, about the unreasonableness of expecting me to come earlier than my appointment time even though I wasn't a new patient and had not been informed beforehand, and the absurdity of turning me away when all I needed was a prescription refill. The doctor was probably sitting in his office idly during the time he had slotted for my appointment. I ended with a declaration that I would never go back there. The receptionist sat there dumbfounded. As much as I wanted to storm out of the office, I had to settle for a quick shuffle. I didn't look back.

I was tired of poor experiences with doctors throughout this ordeal and beforehand, and these doctors were getting away with bad behavior. I would have conversations with doctors where it was clear that they had not bothered to read my chart before stepping into the exam room. They treated me like I was making things up. They treated me impersonally, like I was simply a medical insurance reimbursement and not a person with real needs and concerns. That neurologist knew who his clientele was—many would be in pain or have limited mobility, like me. Where was the compassion?

When I got in the car and drove off, my phone rang. It was the receptionist from the neurologist's office. She apologized and asked me to come back do the doctor could see me. I refused. She offered to call in my prescription refills. I consented. I never went back.

Licensed to Practice

It took me a while to be able to schedule an appointment with the neuromuscular specialist due to changes in my insurance and his full schedule. I finally got an appointment and again I had high hopes about finding a diagnosis. I had browsed his medical research online and his research area appeared to be related to the kind of illness I was experiencing. The doctor's office was located in the medical center. Where I was able to find parking was far from the office building. I said a quick prayer in the car, gathered my strength, and walked to the building. I saw that I still had to take the elevator and trek further to the doctor's office. It's amazing what you're willing to do when you have hope. In the midst of my pain, fatigue, and weakness, I still felt empathy for those who had more difficulty with mobility than I did. Once I got to the office, I checked in with the receptionist, albeit out of breath. I plopped down in a chair and waited. After waiting for quite a while, well past my appointment time, I finally got called back to the exam room.

Sitting on the exam table on top of that noisy white paper always makes me feel like a big kid about to get a shot. My frustration from waiting in the waiting room so long past my appointment began to fade as it was replaced with anxiety and hope about meeting this doctor. A part of me wanted it to go like a movie, or at least an episode of Dr. House. He would come in, take one look at me, tell me that the other doctors who had seen me before and that they should have recognized that I had "insert condition here". He would let me know the treatment and tell me that I would be back to normal in no time. That wasn't how it went.

I didn't have to wait long. The doctor came in, glanced at me, and abruptly started asking me questions. He had a clipboard in his hand, presumably my chart by the way that he kept looking at it. He sat down at a little desk with a computer on it. Once again, I was telling a watered down version of my story. I rushed through it because the look on the doctor's face made it seem as if he really didn't want to hear it. After I finished recounting my experience, he asked the question, "What do you think you have?" I was a little taken aback by this question. After all, that's what I was paying him for. If I wanted my own diagnosis, I could have stayed at home for that and saved myself the anxiety of walking across the medical center parking lot. I replied by spouting off the list of things that the previous doctors had thought I had and later on determined that I didn't. The doctor replied, "That's not what I asked you. I asked you what you thought you had." His retort and tone rubbed me the wrong way. I wasn't sure if I wanted to yell at him or cry instead. After a bit of stammering and stuttering, I told him the condition that the doctor had screened me for before. The results from the tests in the rheumatologist's office were borderline, so I wasn't entirely convinced that it wasn't still an option. He told me, "No, you don't have that. And you need to stop searching on the internet." At that point, I was done with him. Whether his observation was valid or not, his lack of bedside manner (an understatement) was offensive. Little did I know, he was just getting started.

He asked me to get off of the examination table and walk across the room. I did with some difficulty. He asked me to do other things like walk with one foot in front of the other like I was walking on a balance beam and to jump up and down on one foot. I felt like a circus animal on display even though I knew, like the other doctors, he was evaluating my movements. I tried to walk across the room by placing one foot in front of the other and balancing and I couldn't. I almost fell. I started crying. He asked, "Why are your crying?" but the question seemed to be the result of curiosity, not concern. I said calmly, "It's because I used to be able to do things like this before." For a moment, I think my reply softened his heart a bit. He asked me to get back on the table. He stepped out of the room for a moment.

When the doctor returned with his clipboard, he sat down again at the computer desk. He glanced down at the clipboard then looked at me and told me that he did not see any reason for my medical condition and that I needed to reevaluate the stress in my life. He said that he didn't see any reason why I should be taking the medicine that I was taking and that it was probably doing more harm to me than good. He told me that if I felt any better with taking that medicine that it had to be a placebo effect. At that single moment, I hated that man. I hated everything that he stood for that was wrong in the medical field, I hated him for everything that was happening to me, I hated him for his callousness and lack of empathy. He had treated me like an ignorant, uneducated idiot. If I had been a white man, would he have attributed my condition to stress? If I had come in depressed and moping around, would he have believed me?

If he had not walked out of the room so abruptly, I would have yelled in his face. I shuffled out of the room as quickly as my weak body would allow me. Instead of leaving, I returned to the reception desk and asked who I needed to call to report the doctor since his office was part of a larger, well-known medical organization. I wanted them to know how this doctor was marring their prestigious name. I was told that there was a manager on site and that, if I wanted to wait, I could speak with her. I agreed and sat back in the waiting room where I had spent so much time just a half hour earlier. My tears dried and I was only left with brewing anger. After about ten minutes, a woman appeared and called my name. I got ready to get up and she motioned for me to stay seated. She came to me and sat right next to me. She kindly asked what had happened and I explained to her my experience with the doctor. I began to cry again as I told her my story. Her eyes were so kind and sympathetic. When I finished, she alluded to the fact that I was not the first to report this doctor, but because of his prestige and notoriety in the field, they basically had to put up with his bad behavior. She gave me the name of another muscular neurologist that I might want to look up and she assured me that she would file the complaint.

Even though the manager calmed me down for the moment and even though telling the story to her was cathartic, her kindness did not excuse his horrible behavior. He was a prime example of what was wrong in the field of medicine. I believe that, on paper, my case was interesting, appealing, and potentially worthy of a medical journal article. However, once the doctor laid eyes on me, he saw that I didn't look like what my chart said that I should look like and I probably was not a good case for him to bother with from a professional standpoint. I told the manager that they had their very own Dr. House without the charm and she didn't disagree. This was my in-your-face reminder that the world of medicine is a business, not an altruistic, people-serving organization. If there is no personal gain or profit to be attained, then many, including myself, will go without the care and treatment that they need. I believe that is what happened to my mom as well. She was sick for many years before she found a doctor that was willing to believe her and investigate her case thoroughly and relentlessly. By then, it was too late.

I returned home angry and feeling humiliated. I called my mentor who had been dealing with her own medical issues and facing similar circumstances because I knew she would understand what had happened and would be willing to listen to me vent. I told her that I wanted to write a scathing letter to the medical facility about this doctor and write a public online review about him too. I wanted to give up and just let whatever happened to me just happen, even if it meant rolling over and dying. This was my last hope for an answer. I hit a brick wall. I was tired of fighting to only end up with nothing except frustration. She listened, and then told me she had gone through similar circumstances. She encouraged me to not think about this as starting over. "You just need a new team of doctors," she said. She was optimistic and she was right, but I had still given up.

The Root Cause

Despite the muscular neurologist's poor bedside manner and offensive delivery of his medical opinion, I couldn't help but to consider what he said. Had I done this to myself? Even though I was currently far less stressed, had my prolonged stress from the previous ten years activated something irreparable in my body? I also thought about the placebo effect. Even though I knew this was not a placebo effect, I wondered what would happen if I stopped my regimented doses of medicine.

I returned to my primary care physician and told her what the muscular neurologist had said. I also told her that I wanted to stop taking my medicine to see what would happen. She was supportive, but advised me to wean myself off of it rather than quitting cold turkey. I took her advice and reduced my three-doses-a-day to two. I was prepared for the worse, but nothing happened. After a week of only taking two doses, I reduced my intake to one dose a day of the medicine for my muscles and stopped taking the medicine for my nerves altogether. After all, the tingling and numbness in my hands, arms, and feet were annoying and slightly painful, but not unbearable. Again I prepared for the worse. I slowed down in my movements slightly, but I did not end up incapacitated as I had been before. After another week of only one dose, I stopped taking the medicine completely. I was nervous! I carried doses of the medicine in my purse as I had always done out of fear that I would be out somewhere in public when my legs would give out, but it didn't happen. I began testing my limits by walking farther than I normally would and becoming more active. I still had to take naps daily and rest frequently, but I couldn't believe my progress!

Throughout this ordeal, I had begun to renew my faith and zeal for God. My story of illness and road to recovery became my testimony. By His stripes I was healed and this sickness would not come upon me a second time was the promise that I held onto. For a while, I had the half-full prescription bottles as a testament to my recovery. Later, I realized that hanging onto those medicines was a crutch, a "just in case something happened" safety net, so I threw them away. I am still mindful of my body's signals—I know when to slow down, when to rest, and when to stop. I am still in pain many days, but I am so much better. Every morning when I open my eyes, I start by wiggling my toes, and then I praise God. Then I roll out of bed and thank God as my feet hit the floor and I stand under my own strength without holding onto anything. He is my comfort, my Healer, and my Strength!

I never received a name for what it was I went through. There is no way to know how the malfunctions in my body will present themselves in the future. What I do know is that God allowed me to get still and to seek Him, even if I had to be flat on my back to do it. He brought me back to Him and healed my body, my mind, and my faith.

Get Well Soon

I did not publicize my illness. There were no postings on social media and I did not sent out group texts to friends and acquaintances. Those who knew me well were aware that I had been in the hospital and that my quality of life had been significantly diminished. When I heard from someone I had not talked to in a while and gave them an abridged version of my ordeal, the responses were generally the same: an expression of sympathy followed by "get well soon". When the shoe was on the other foot, I behaved in the same way toward those who were ill, but as the sick person, I really began to contemplate what get well soon means to a person who has a life-threatening or chronic illness.

One of the most frustrating aspects of my experience was the possibility that I would not receive an answer regarding what was attacking my body. I believed that the illness had to be named in order to be defeated. It did not make sense that I could experience an illness that no one had ever experienced before. That seemed impossible. How could I get well if I did not even have an answer as to what I had? I was tired of dead ends and I did not have the strength to start over. I was not optimistic enough to believe that a new team of doctors would be any more successful in diagnosing and treating me, especially if I had seen the "best" already.

The reports from the doctors made it seem as if I were dealing with a chronic issue. My life would be forever changed and I would have to learn to deal with the presence of this illness in my life. It was difficult to fathom being exhausted all the time and barely being able to care for myself, much less my children. At my age, I knew that I should expect more life ahead of me than behind me but the illness made me doubt the truth of that. Even if it were true, I wasn't sure that I wanted to live that life. On the other hand, as I weaned myself off of the medication, I wondered whether my condition was acute. Maybe it was a temporary affliction that left just as mysteriously as it came. I still don't know the answer to that question and every time I have an ache or pain or feel sluggish in the afternoon, an overwhelming feeling of dread comes over me and I wonder whether my condition was indeed chronic and is returning once again. Only time will tell. With every checkup and doctor's visit, I look less and less like the kind of person who has been through what my medical chart says.

The more time that passes since the onset of my mysterious illness, the more it feels surreal. I have to remind myself that it was not a dream or even a nightmare, but a real experience that I, along with my family, experienced. I remember before my hospital visit I always wondered if I was crazy. The long list of symptoms did not seem to add up to anything substantial initially. Since my mom died due to an autoimmune disease and her symptoms had largely been ignored until they became life-threatening, I was determined not to let anyone make me believe I was crazy for noticing what was not right with my body. However, without a diagnosis, I again wondered if I was crazy and somehow all of this was a manifestation of my mind and associated stress. Despite those moments of doubt and what anyone else may say, I know that I am quite sane and that none of what I felt and experience was imaginary.

Lessons Learned

I may never know or understand what happened to me. All I know is that my body betrayed me. The good news is that I learned from my experience. I learned that I can no longer be superwoman. Being a workaholic and carrying around everyone else's problems on top of my own almost cost me my life. Since then, I have learned to treasure sleep, energy, and movement in my body. I work out when I can and take it easy when I have to. For the longest, I would wake up in the morning, lie still on my back, and wiggle my toes, just to make sure that I could. Now, you can't keep up with me! Looking at me now, you would never know that I went through this battle. But I know. Every time I feel a bit of weakness in my body, a tingle in my hands, or the pain in my hip, I wonder if today is the day that it all gets taken away from me again. That thought doesn't bring me down though. It inspires me to make the most of every day that I get to live and to move! I am not angry or upset that this happened to me. In reality, I am thankful. So many blessings fell upon me because of this break in my life. Had I kept going on the path that I was headed, I would have delayed or, even worse, never realized the potential that is within me.

About the Authors

Amber E. Williams

Amber E. Williams has over 15 years of experience in the field of education and is state-certified as a teacher and principal. She has worked in traditional public schools as well as charter schools and has served in the roles of classroom teacher, Dean of Instruction, Assistant Principal, and Principal. She has a B.A. in English and an MBA.

Amber E. Williams is the owner and CEO of Williams Education Consulting and the author of Discover Your Path to Leadership. Williams specializes in transformative leadership coaching and is passionate about helping leaders to grow. She can be contacted for leadership coaching, writing projects, and public speaking engagements at www.amberewilliams.com.

awilliams@amberewilliams.com
www.amberewilliams.com
http://amberewilliams.com/leadership-tips
Twitter: @amberonthemove
www.facebook.com/amberewilliams

Gigi Brown

Goldia "Gigi" Brown is an author, speaker, and New Thought practitioner. With a commitment and passion for developing, encouraging and empowering all people. Goldia is on a mission to assist each individual to both grow their potential and use their gifts to contribute to society's well-being.

Following the teachings of world renowned New Thought Spiritual Leader, Bishop Dr. Barbara Lewis King, Goldia contributes Dr. Barbara with inspiring her to answer the call to be a servant leader. Blending New Thought principles with her training and expertise in leadership, Goldia delivers writings, talks, and trainings that celebrate the beauty and inherent greatness of each individual.

Goldia "Gigi" Brown is also a John Maxwell coach, speaker, and trainer who holds two degrees in Leadership (Brenau University (BA) and Mercer University (MS). Writing under the pen name of Gigi Brown, Goldia is the author of *"The Courage to Sit."*

Brittany A. Daniel, LPC

Brittany Daniel is a licensed professional counselor who has been servicing the greater Houston area for over four years. She is the owner of Voice Counseling and Life Skills, a private counseling practice dedicated to helping others become the best version of themselves. Extending beyond the office, she is the founder of the "Wear the Crown Retreat," a community outreach initiative that promotes mental, emotional, and physical wellness among young girls. Most recently, she has combined her passion for helping others with her love for writing by publishing her first book, "Love, Happiness, and all that other Sh*t", in 2017. She encourages women to identify and access the power they have to create change and ultimately live a life fulfilled. Brittany Daniel is a testament to the idea that capability overrides circumstance and she hopes to instill that sentiment with all whom she encounters.

To connect further with Brittany visit www.voicecounseling.org or follow @b.daniel_lpc on Instagram.

Lakichay Nadira Muhammad

Affectionately known as "The Queen of Self Improvement" aka "The Wellness Angel", Lakichay Nadira Muhammad has an extensive background in the healing arts. This international bestselling author, speaker, and life and wellness strategist is committed to the awakening and refinement of the original woman.

As a "Wholistic" Health Practitioner, Lakichay Nadira prides herself on helping her clients obtain optimal health and wellness through mental, physical, spiritual, and emotional alignment. Lakichay Nadira's extensive trainings and background affords her the opportunity to transform the lives of communities. With a love for health, community development, real estate investing, and permaculture, this business owner, wife and mother has effectively learned how to marry her unique gifts and talents to serve the greater good of the community.

Lakichay Nadira can be found breathing and speaking life into the hearts and minds of the people that she was put here to serve.

www.LakichayNadirah.com
www.TheCenterforSelfImprovement.com

Njeri Watkins

Njeri Watkins is a Lecturer, Digital Intelligence Consultant and Instructor at the University of British Columbia | Sauder School of Business - Executive Education. For the past two decades she has developed and taught programs on Leadership, Communications, Personal Branding and Marketing Strategy for academic institutions, government training programs, community organizations and professional associations.

Njeri's extensive background in digital media, business development and facilitation has expanded to the development of her signature programs: Demystifying Digital Analytics and Digital Due Diligence Solutions.

Njeri is an active contributor in the community as Speaker, Advisor and Startup Mentor with multiple business accelerators and leadership programs as well as Co-Chair for the Digital Analytics Association – Vancouver Chapter. Njeri passionately supports others in actualizing their highest potential as a Self-Management Leader with the University of Victoria - Institute on Aging and Lifelong Health.

Instagram: @njeriwatkins
Twitter: @njeriwatkins
linkedin: ca.linkedin.com/in/njeriwatkins
website: www.njeri.ca
email: info@njeri.ca

Contributing Authors

Krystal Humphrey

Krystal D. Humphrey, M.A., LPC, CART is a practicing, licensed professional counselor (LPC) and the proprietor of Imani Counseling Services PLLC located in Houston, TX. Ms. Humphrey attended Sam Houston State University in Huntsville, TX where she completed her bachelor's degree in psychology and a Master's in counseling. She is also certified in anger management and pre/post marital counseling through Prepare Enrich.

Star Parker

Tsi Tsi Parker is the CEO of Tsi Tsi P. Productions and founder of The Parker VII Foundation which both produce various works of art created to inspire and empower others. Through different challenges of her own, she found art to be therapeutic and stands by the philosophy that our needs are often met by meeting the needs of others. As a writer, mentor and public speaker, she developed a passion to educate and elevate others, helping them to reach their highest potential.

Alycia Richard

Alycia M. Richard holds a master's degree in Public Administration and is Green Belt Certified in Lean Six Sigma. She has worked in the healthcare industry for over ten years and specializes in organizational development. Alycia is passionate about implementing processes that drive organizations forward by enhancing employee engagement and enhancing customer satisfaction. Alycia is the proud mother of Jaiden and Jacob Grace who constantly keep her on the go. She enjoys serving at her church and a good Netflix binge and is learning to play golf.

Dr. Temeca L. Richardson

Dr. Temeca Richardson (Dr. T) is a personal transformation coach and professional educator who provides solutions and valuable insight to inspire and encourage women to love themselves more. Dr. T has dedicated her life's work to supporting high-performing women who have depression, who find it difficult to put themselves first, and those who are constantly asking, 'what am I doing/why am I here?' Yes, you CAN live with no regrets even while focusing on you.

www.ingramcontent.com/pod-product-compliance
Lightning Source LLC
LaVergne TN
LVHW041617070426
835507LV00008B/296